COACHING PERSPECTIVES VI

Center for Coaching Certification

Cathy Liska

Kaleen Barbera

Betsy Laughter

Jennifer Maxwell Parkinson

Shaddae Renee

Amanda Quayle

Julie Kratz

Linda Clark

Emily Bass

Kelly Gangl

Cheryl Knight

Juanita Bulloch

Copyright © 2016 by the Center for Coaching Certification LLC

All rights reserved. No part of this publication may be reproduced, distributed, or transmitted in any form or by any means, including photocopying, recording, or other electronic or mechanical methods without the prior written permission of the publisher, except in the case of brief quotations embodied in critical reviews and certain other noncommercial uses permitted by copyright law. For permission requests, write to Info@CenterforCoachingCertification.com.

Full rights to the individual chapters in this book are granted to the respective author for their use, and they may grant rights to their individual chapters as they deem appropriate.

Names and identifying details have been changed to protect the privacy of individuals.

The authors and publisher have made every effort to ensure accuracy and completeness of the information in this book. We assume no responsibility for errors, inaccuracies, omissions, or any inconsistencies herein. Any slights of people, places, or organizations are unintentional. Although the authors and publisher have made every effort to ensure that the information in this book was correct at press time, the authors and publisher do not assume and hereby disclaim any liability to any party for any loss, damage, or disruption, either direct or indirect, caused by errors or omissions, whether such errors or omissions result from negligence, accident, or any other cause.

The information in this book is meant to supplement, not replace, proper coaching training. Like any profession, coaching requires training.

Dear Reader,

Each year a group of brilliant Certified Professional and Certified Master Coaches collaborate to write the next book for the Coaching Perspectives series. It is an honor to work with these graduates as they share their expertise.

The chapters in this book are individual reads and the combination is powerful for coaches and clients alike. The tips, techniques, and tools shared support your success.

Enjoy your journey as coach and/or coachee, taking time to reflect on how you want to apply the insights here for your continued forward progress and success.

Kindly let us know how we can be helpful.

Sincerely,

Cathy Liska
Cathy Liska
Guide from the Side®
Center for Coaching Certification

CENTER FOR COACHING CERTIFICATION

www.CenterforCoachingCertification.com

Info@CenterforCoachingCertification.com

800-350-1678

MISSION:

Enhance your coach training experience with quality, professionalism, and support.

VISION:

A high-quality, ethical norm throughout the coaching profession achieved through leadership by example.

Table of Contents

The Journey to Become a Coach *by Cathy Liska*....................…….....1

Crossroads of Manager, Trainer, and Coach *by Kaleen Barbera*...25

Coaching from the Heart *by Betsy Laughter*………...…………….45

Coaching: The Total Package *by Jennifer Maxwell Parkinson*......63

Mapping Your Dream *by Shaddae Renee*…………...…..…………..83

Career Coaching for Students *by Amanda Quayle*……………........103

Career Game Plans *by Julie Krat*………...…………….................123

When It Is Time for Feedback *by Linda Clark*……………......……141

Coaching the Athlete Versus the Executive *by Emily Bass*……..164

How Coaching Helped a Legacy Business *by Kelly Gangl*……...186

The HR Leader's Transition to Coach *by Cheryl Knight*…..........205

Affirmation for Sustainable Change *by Juanita Bulloch*…..........225

*For coaches,
those thinking about becoming a coach,
and those who receive coaching.*

THE JOURNEY TO BECOME A COACH
Cathy Liska

Coaching is more than an up and coming profession - coaching is a way of being.

Coaching as a way of being means a positive, proactive attitude and approach to people, conversations, and challenges.

> *Coaching as a way of being means a positive, proactive attitude and approach to people, conversations, and challenges.*

While many call themselves a coach without embarking on the journey that starts with training, the journey is what makes a coach. Being a coach means learning the coaching competencies, living by the Code of Ethics, and applying the science of coaching in coaching sessions.

What is the journey to become a professional coach? Similar to other professions, becoming a coach starts with education, ethics, and then skill as a coach grows with experience. This chapter is about the journey to becoming a coach.

What education or training is required? There is self-regulation within coaching that is expanding the savvy around how to coach and the awareness of the importance for standards. At the forefront of this is the International Coach Federation,

ICF, and their requirement for membership is 60 hours of coach specific training. Some mistakenly say that training is unnecessary. After all, professional service providers must know what they are doing and must be ethical – right? The biggest challenge to the coaching profession is people who call themselves a coach without training. Additionally, the media often miss-portray coaching. Some well-known public figures call themselves a coach without knowing what coaching means. Well-intentioned individuals are using the word coach and are in reality doing therapy without a license or serving as a consultant instead of a coach. It is incumbent on trained coaches to increase the awareness of coach training, ethics, and standards. The self-regulation within coaching that is expanding the savvy around how to coach and the awareness of the standards.

How often, when hiring a professional, have you assumed that the person you are hiring was required to have training and follow ethical guidelines? Think about your doctor, dentist, counselor, financial planner, accountant, minister, massage therapist, sports coach, or personal trainer. Are you willing to hire one of these professionals if they have no training? Every profession has standards and this includes coaching.

Do you want an untrained coach? Even if they are a famous figure or well-known coach – do you want them as your coach if they have zero training as a coach? Do you want a coach who is not accountable to a Code of Ethics?

WHAT IS COACHING?

The definition of coaching from the International Coach Federation, ICF, the self-regulating body of the coaching profession, includes language that demonstrates both how coaching is different from other roles and what it really involves. The ICF defines coaching as a strategic partnership. This is different in that other professional service providers are considered the expert while the coach provides a process. A coach partners with individual clients who are recognized as their own best expert. The definition goes on to say that the coach empowers the client. This is very different from enabling, advising, or directing. The coach is the supporting partner for an individual to be their best self. The definition explains that the client clarifies their own goals, creates their own action plans, plans moving past their obstacles, and ultimately achieves what they, the client, choose.

> *A coach partners with individual clients who are recognized as their own best expert.*

What is the role of the coach? The coach listens, rephrases, and asks powerful questions. The coach is a sounding board to expand thinking, challenge ideas, explore perspectives, develop strategies, and ultimately serve as an accountability partner for the client to move forward. Moving forward is an essential underpinning; coaches focus on the future.

Before I really understood coaching, I had people asking me if I was willing to coach them. Others recommended that I be a coach. My knowledge of coaching was limited to sports coaching or more of a consulting approach. Because I misunderstood coaching, I figured I was capable and I liked the idea. Eventually when someone asked me to be their coach I said yes. While I was unsure of what I was doing, I dove in whole-heartedly and with great intentions.

It was much like if I were a medical doctor and someone asked me to be their psychiatrist. While there are some transferable skills it really is a very different service. Think about it this way: do you want your dentist to do your annual physical? After all, they have many transferable skills. A more common misunderstanding is a mental health professional serving as a coach without coach specific training. A mental health professional has many transferable skills and at the same time coaching is completely different from mental health services. Sometimes people, well-known or otherwise, call themselves coaches and then act as an unlicensed mental health professional.

Here are explanations of the different roles that are most often mistakenly interchanged with coaching:
- Mentor – an individual with experience who guides another, passing on their wisdom.
- Consultant – an expert who analyzes the circumstances, develops a plan for change, and provides advice.

- Trainer – a subject matter expert who teaches specific content based on the determination of requirements.
- Facilitator – a guide for a specified group of people to reach a pre-determined objective.
- Mental Health Professional – a licensed counselor, therapist, psychologist, psychiatrist, or social worker who assesses, diagnoses, and prescribes a course of action.
- Human Resources – a trained professional who manages the various aspects of hiring, supporting, and supervising a work force.
- Manager or Supervisor – a specific person who oversees and directs others to meet objectives and complete tasks.

In contrast, a coach is trained in a specific process to partner with individuals as they explore their possibilities and challenges, create strategies, plan actions, and move toward their objectives. A trained coach recognizes their client is their own best expert and empowers them by applying coaching competencies and the coaching process.

COACHING BEFORE TRAINING

Before coach training, when clients asked me to coach, I thought I knew how to be helpful and I even thought I knew how to coach. Big mistake! Basically I was a mentor; I managed to ask a few decent questions and I gave advice. As I have since learned, I got in the way of my clients' success by being too involved in finding the answer and by asking weak questions.

What is the lesson to be learned? Coaching truly is a profession with competencies, ethics, standards, and a science-based process. When done properly it has an average return on investment of 600% according to Fortune magazine. Wow! In terms of being a professional, training is an essential and ethical approach.

PERSONAL ROI OF COACHING

One great example of the personal ROI of coaching is a client who engaged in coaching because they had a new boss and were in conflict. Through the coaching process they explored different perspectives of their interactions with the new boss and different approaches for making it work. The client then developed a strategy with specific action steps on how to make their workplace relationship work. As a result, the client effectively changed their relationship with their boss so their interactions became proactive and the work environment positive.

On the surface the ROI seems clear – the client saved their job. It goes deeper. For the individual client it meant maintaining their income level because it saved them from a job search for the same position, likely at a lower rate of pay. It also meant the client and their family were spared from relocation. This impacted their family because the client's spouse was able to stay in their job and the children were able to stay in their school. It also impacted others at work because it meant the office was more positive and functional.

COACHING DEFINED EXPLAINS HIGH ROI

Coaching is a unique profession with unique processes that provide amazing results. The oft-cited Manchester Inc. study states the ROI is 529% which is right in line with a multitude of additional studies including Metrix Global. This is far and above other services and processes. Based on the various studies on coaching and the impact, it begs the question: how can anyone afford to miss out on having a coach? Coaching is an amazing tool!

> *How can anyone afford to miss out on having a coach?*

How does coaching provide such an incredible return on investment? Think back to the definition provided earlier and compare that to what normally happens at home, at work, or with friends. Unfortunately, many of us have the mistaken idea that helping means telling the answer. Realistically, when someone is told the answer, how often do they follow through? Hmm; rarely. When people figure out their own answer, that is when they follow through. Coaching it is all about empowering the client for their own exploration and discovery. In this way the client owns their answer and gets the results.

The caveat: is this true for all coaching? Unfortunately, no. The journey to coaching with training and ethics makes a difference, client engagement makes a difference, and the top indicator of success is the rapport between coach and client.

To be a coach start by learning about training options. Research coaching, the ICF, and what it means to be a professional coach.

RESEARCHING AND LEARNING ABOUT TRAINING

Because I made mistakes when coaching without training, I wanted help. I researched online for six months. After completing a coach training program that seemed to make sense, I got even more involved with the coaching profession. Then I learned more. I learned about the ICF and visited their website at www.CoachFederation.org. There I learned about coaching competencies and ethics. The training I had lacked approval and others started telling me about additional concerns. This inspired more research and learning, and the launch of the Center for Coaching Certification to ensure quality, affordability, effective training, and immediate applicability of the content.

When researching options and choosing a coaching certification program, be sure the training is approved by the ICF. Check to make sure all eleven core competencies are covered and that the program provides both coaching tools and follow-up support.

WHAT HAPPENS IN COACH TRAINING?

Coach training ideally is designed to develop the 11 Core Competencies of a coach. Programs vary, so what follows is drawn from the Center for Coaching Certification.

Coach training explores types of coaching, what a coach is not, what a coach is, plus discussion similar to what happens when coaches talk with prospective clients. The Code of Ethics calls for agreements to explain the roles; establishing an agreement starts with a conversation and then moves to a written agreement.

Coaching is different from psychology, psychiatry, counseling, therapy, or social work. Those professions require separate training and licensing. Mental health professionals diagnose, address problems from the past, and provide direction. Practicing without a license is illegal and there are cases where people claiming to coach were actually practicing mental health.

A coach is neither a mentor, an advisor, a consultant, a teacher, nor a friend. Each of these roles calls for giving advice.

Note: it is possible to coach a friend depending on the relationship and the boundaries established for coaching.

There are situations where serving in more than one role benefits the client if handled properly. This requires advance planning and an agreement.

A coach is a sounding board to expand and challenge the thinking of the client. A coach asks questions to explore perspective and focus. A coach empowers the client to develop their strategy. A coach serves as an accountability partner and a motivation partner.

In keeping with the 11 Core Competencies, learning and ultimately being accountable to a Code of Ethics is essential. There are five sections in the ICF Code of Ethics:

- **Professional Conduct at Large**: As professionals, coaches are called upon to accurately portray their experience and education, respect the contributions of others, and know their own limits.
- **Conflicts of Interest**: Coaches avoid conflicts of interest and when one arises disclose it so the client is aware and has choices.
- **Professional Conduct with Clients**: Beginning a coaching relationship with honest insight as to coaching outcomes, the boundaries and the freedoms, and the nature of the

coaching relationship covered in a clear agreement supports long-term success.

- **Confidentiality/Privacy**: Confidentiality is paramount in coaching so the Code of Ethics provides for protection of the client by ensuring all records are confidential and protected, and that there is agreement with the client before releasing any information.
- **Continuing Development:** The Code of Ethics calls for coaches to commit to their own ongoing development.

Different people think, feel, and prioritize differently. Because a coach is called upon to understand the client and to be present in the moment, recognizing how the client thinks, feels, and prioritizes in the moment provides tremendous value and benefit.

> *Different people think, feel, and prioritize differently.*

The coaching competencies in communication are listening, powerful questioning, and clear, direct language. Coaches are called upon to challenge themselves because these are skills to work on continuously.

- When the listener rephrases and reflects, the speaker knows they are heard and understood, plus the listener is improving their own skills.
- The words we use significantly impact understanding, focus, and outcomes. Choosing words that say what we

do want instead of what we don't want seems simple; it requires practice.
- "Do you think you should...?" isn't really a question, it is expressing an opinion. The way questions are asked determines the flow of the conversation. Coaching questions are clarifying, probing, advice-free, and open-ended. Tips for formulating questions include:
    o KISS: Keep It Short and Simple
    o Ask questions that focus forward
    o Ask questions that are open to possibilities
    o If the client is logical, ask thinking questions
    o If the client relies on their instincts, ask feeling questions
    o Ask one question at a time
    o The answer often leads to the next question
    o Use 'What' or 'How' questions

Keep It Short and Simple

Coaching competencies include creating awareness, designing actions, planning and goal setting, plus managing accountability.

The way a client uses language provides the coach with insight. For example, because of how much information we process every day, we delete, distort, or generalize to manage the amount of information. Training provides the insight on how to identify this and ask more questions.

Language also indicates focus.
- When a client focuses on what they don't want, the coach will ask them about what they *do* want.
- When motivated externally, the client defers to others or outside factors. The coach will then explore what it means to the client personally to get the result.
- If a client is waiting on others or circumstance before taking action, their language includes such phrases as "after they do this" or "when that happens". The coach asks what actions the client does control now to support the desired outcome.

Practice during coach training and experience coaching enhances the skills of the coach. Training on coaching process makes this easier and provides a methodology for results. The coaching practicum during training provides both a process and practice.

Coaching skills and process lead to effective coaching. For those interested in having a coaching business, more is required. For example, at the Center for Coaching Certification the coach login page provides business and marketing tools in addition to the myriad of coaching tools. Ongoing support is also available after the coach training with additional training options, free monthly webinars for continuing education, opportunities to attract coaching work through an online directory, the chance to be published in this book series, and more.

Coach training develops the coaching competencies, provides techniques and tools, and creates a network of colleagues in addition to access for ongoing support.

How Much Training?

If you research training you can find hundreds of options ranging from a few hours to ten years or even more. The ICF requires 60 hours of coach specific training to become a member. In addition to membership, the ICF offers credentialing at three levels. If you want to become a coach, at a minimum plan on qualifying for ICF membership (which is much like earning a degree or certification in any profession). Then, much like choosing to earn a masters or doctorate, credentialing with the ICF means advanced training and paid experience as a coach.

> *If you want to become a coach, at a minimum plan on qualifying for ICF membership...*

The ICF approves training programs.
- One approach for ICF-approved training is an all-in-one commitment to sixty hours of training plus mentor coaching plus you remain a student while you are coaching for the hundred hours required to earn the first level of credentialing.

- A different approach is a-la-carte with ICF-approved programs of 30 or more hours that you combine as you choose based on your budget and schedule. This means earning a certification in that program and returning for the additional hours and an additional level of certification. When you want to earn a credential you also choose the timing of your mentor coaching. This is typically more affordable.

With the a-la-carte approach to coach training, some participants of the first 30 hours of coach training are coaching within other jobs, or learning coaching to apply in other roles. Often this broadens the perspectives and range of expertise of the class participants.

For people who offer their services as a professional coach, qualifying for membership in the ICF and joining are a must.

WHAT KIND OF TRAINING?

Because there are hundreds of options for coach training, a checklist for the programs you consider is helpful:
- ICF Approved – a must!
- CEUs – many professional roles or designations require earning continuing education units and a program that is accredited for this adds value to your training.

- Schedule – when and where are the classes? How does that fit with your schedule and location?
- Cost – how much and how is it paid?
- Tools and Resources – what additional tools and resources are provided to graduates?
- Support – what ongoing support is available?

WHAT INFORMATION IS IMPORTANT IN TRAINING?

Because a professional coach is deeply engaged with the work and life of their client, learning the ICF's 11 Core Competencies of a coach is preparation for offering coaching services. Many coaches have a high level of experience and education before transitioning to coaching. An effective training program builds on existing knowledge and provides perspective on the difference in applying skills as a coach versus in other roles.

The Core Competencies identified by ICF include:
1. Meeting Ethical Guidelines and Professional Standards
2. Establishing the Coaching Agreement
3. Establishing Trust and Intimacy with the Client
4. Coaching Presence
5. Active Listening
6. Powerful Questioning
7. Direct Communication
8. Creating Awareness

9. Designing Actions
10. Planning and Goal Setting
11. Managing Progress and Accountability

When choosing a coach training program, ensure that all eleven of these competencies are developed. Continue developing these competencies through ongoing learning and practice.

When hiring a coach, verifying their training and membership in the ICF is smart.

> *When hiring a coach, verifying their training and membership in the ICF is smart.*

MY JOURNEY TO COACHING

How does anyone decide to become a coach? This question is often asked of me too: how did I decide to become a coach and to offer coach training?

In many ways the journey started long before I heard the term coaching as it applies to being a business, career, life, wellness, or executive coach. The concept of empowering others was something I learned from my family. My parents modeled it by encouraging and supporting each of us to find and explore our own path in life.

As a young adult in the working world, I experienced the difference between a manager that empowered and a manager that micro managed. It is fairly easy to figure out which approach is more effective in the long run. When I moved into management myself, in addition to realizing empowering employees was more effective in terms of their engagement; it also created better bottom line results and a more positive company culture.

> *... the difference between a manager that empowered and a manager that micro managed. It is fairly easy to figure out which approach is more effective in the long run.*

The positions I held were varied because initially it was about supporting my children as a single mom and later because I became a military spouse and relocated several times. On the con side it was challenging and there was a lot of change. On the pro side I learned so much, had wide exposure to different types of work and people, and became adept at flexing with the changes. In each position I was very focused on what people wanted and how what I did supported their goals.

As I subsequently learned, a coach is focused on empowering their client. Coach training teaches us about partnering with people in a way that empowers them to create their own success. This had proven true in my experience.

As an example, at one time I hired a manager for an apartment community who was living in a shelter. She had the skill set and simply wanted a chance. By giving her that chance I earned a loyal team member who did an amazing job.

In a restaurant I owned for a time I learned how adapting to individuals appropriately created positivity on the whole team. We had a cook who required accommodation for height to reach the stove and the walk-in freezer. It was easy to do and it gained so much in terms of employee engagement.

In a nonprofit I provided financial counseling services and training classes. When the process was focused on the individual choosing their own budget and actions, it empowered them so they successfully paid their debts and saved money.

In another position I helped clients create and grow nonprofit organizations. The focus was on what they wanted the organization to be and to offer in the community. The successes continue to this day because it truly was their success.

Because I was a mom and a military spouse, I started working for myself for the flexibility. One day my husband shared a write-up on mediation and mediation training. The idea of learning techniques for supporting people to take charge of their own decisions was exciting. I became certified in conflict mediation empowering people to figure out how they want to handle their conflicts.

Eventually I became a trainer and travelled all around the country. During this time, I learned how much sense it made for people to learn about effective communication techniques. The classes I gave on management, team building, and what was called coaching gave me an opportunity to pull my experiences together and truly solidify my own knowledge. During this time people asked me if I was willing to coach them. I really did not know what they meant. After being asked multiple times and having people suggest I become a coach, I figured it was time to learn more about this coaching thing. As a result, my research refocused my thinking on how much sense coaching makes and how coaching is a natural extension of my philosophy. The next step was obvious; I attended coaching certification and started coaching.

Coach training was an eye opener. Because learning about coaching was so powerful, I wanted to teach it too and became a certified coach trainer. Teaching coaching led to learning even more about the work. Ultimately I learned that for the coaching profession it is incredibly important that coaches have standards and ethics. The gold standard for coach training is the International Coach Federation, ICF, because they have the standards for membership, the 11 Core Competencies, the Code of Ethics, a process for approving coach training, accountability for member coaches, a process for credentialing, and wide recognition - all the elements that have legitimized a multitude of other professions. Understanding the importance of specific content for coach training and student feedback helped build the foundation of the Center for Coaching Certification. The coaching certification focuses on quality and professionalism plus providing support.

How Does Coaching Really Work?

To simplify the process, a coach invites the client to determine their objectives and what they want from the coaching. The coach sets the foundation by discussing both coaching and client interests, and then providing the client with a written agreement and access to the Code of Ethics. During sessions the coach asks the client what they want to focus on, listens, asks the client about barriers and options, explores strategies, and asks the client for their action plan. The coach will probe and clarify, rephrase, challenge, expand thinking, and support forward progress. The coach is truly a partner for the client and empowers the client to be their own best expert.

What is the Process to Become a Coach?

The steps for becoming a professional coach are:
1. Find and enroll in a coach training program that is approved by the International Coach Federation.

2. Engage fully in all class discussions, homework assignments, and practice coaching.
3. Review class materials and practice what you learn to increase your retention.
4. Complete the 60 hours of training required for membership with the ICF and join.
5. Participate fully in continuing education both because it is required and to further enhance your skills.
6. Advance your credibility further by pursuing credentialing with the ICF.
7. If you are coaching inside of a company support the coaching program OR if you are starting your own business as a coach learn about business and marketing to effectively create your infrastructure and offer coaching.

Being a coach is a continuous learning process and an ongoing journey. It is a privilege to embark on the journey and experience the learning, to be coached and coach during training.

Being hired to coach others is an honor and a responsibility. Accept the gift graciously, authentically, and with great care for the value of the coaching relationship.

Cathy Liska is founder and CEO of the Center for Coaching Certification and the Center for Coaching Solutions. As the Guide from the Side®, she is recognized among the best in training, coaching, conflict management, and consulting. Cathy has presented, trained, and facilitated thousands of events, workshops, certification courses, and organizational retreats.

Cathy has earned the following designations: Certified Master Coach Trainer, Certified Master Coach, Certified Consumer Credit Counselor, Real Estate Broker, Certified Apartment Manager, Certified Family Mediator, Certified Civil Mediator, Certificate of Excellence in Nonprofit Leadership and Management, Certification in the Drucker Self-Assessment Tool, Grief Support Group Facilitator, and Certified Trainer/Facilitator.

Her three coaching niche areas include Business Development, Communication and Conflict, and Intentional Choices. Cathy balances training other coaches, coaching up to 12 individual clients at a time, writing and publishing, and volunteering.

Cathy's personal mission statement is "People". Focused on empowering others, Cathy is known for her passion to support others achieving the results they desire.

Cathy@CenterforCoachingCertification.com

CROSSROADS OF MANAGING, TRAINING, AND COACHING

Kaleen A. Barbera

WHAT TO EXPECT

If you are reading this book, chances are you have many of your own coaching insights and also may be looking to improve or gather information that helps you be a more effective professional. I have been fortunate enough to experience the roles of manager, trainer, and coach over the last 20 years. As I reflect on my history, as well as observations of others, some things stand out. In this chapter I will take a closer look at each role and hopefully provide the reader an even greater awareness as to which hat to wear and the benefits of knowing how the roles are unique to one another. If we want to be better managers, coaches, and trainers, one way of doing that is to access information from various perspectives.

> *If we want to be better managers, coaches, and trainers, one way of doing that is to access information from various perspectives.*

I've chosen to take a deeper dive into these three roles specifically because, through my career as a consultant, I recognize these are the roles most often responsible for the development of other professionals. The attributes of each role vary; how do they overlap? What unique functions provide impact in different and beneficial ways? It seems there are some obvious answers, and as I continue to train and coach managers, their staff, and also other trainers, I realize that it is still unclear.

The effectiveness of each of these roles and the tendency to act more like one than another is, at times, based on the responses and behavior of the individual being managed, coached, or trained. There is certainly a dynamic between individuals that can create a reaction whether or not it was intended. While that may be the case, here we are solely focused on the person in the role in question, and the actions within their control.

I Learned More Than Geometry in High School

When I was in high school my mom, a high school teacher, highly recommended (translation = told me) that in order for me to get accepted into a good university, I had to be well rounded. What she meant was that since the only activity that occupied my time outside of school was riding my horse, and since most schools weren't looking to admit brainy, horseback riding-obsessed teenagers, I better get signed up for some recognizable activities to round out my academic career. I went on to join quite a few after school activities and although I was extremely busy, I discovered that I was really good at several of them. One that became my passion was photography.

My newfound love of photography led me to earn the position of Photo Editor of our high school newspaper. In that role, I had the distinct honor of working with the teacher designated to manage the newspaper and its team, Carolyn Brown. Mrs. Brown was a southern woman: congenial, spoke with a twang, had a warm heart, and an easy laugh. When we had to get to business, she put us to task. We absolutely loved doing our jobs for the newspaper and she was a key ingredient of our overall team's happiness. We were fine with working our tails off for each edition. So the questions I ask myself are: what was it she did that made us want to do so well? Did I consider her a coach, a manager, a trainer, or all or none of these?

> *... what was it she did that made us want to do so well?*

When helping people become their best selves, based on my experience, those are really the ultimate questions. Is mastering any one of those roles the key? Or is it a combination of all three? At different times, what is appropriate? Where do they intersect and how can we be most effective at each? This chapter is a reflection and study in how each functional role is defined and the benefits of understanding what role you play naturally, offering awareness of where improvement provides the most benefit.

The Manager

I define a manager as someone who has been given authority to deal with people and tasks at a given business or company. How do they execute and use that authority? How they use their authority in the best way is often unclear. That is the one of the reasons that managers seek help. Let's take a look at some of the challenges of identifying the role of manager.

When I graduated college, I decided to start a career in retail management. The training program required approximately one year of intense learning, on and off the sales floor, to fully understand what was required to be promoted to the role of manager. There was an assistant manager who rarely smiled so employees didn't consider her a friend or even friendly. She gave very little praise or positive reinforcement, was a task master, and made us do things so she didn't have to do them herself. As a result, many of us felt a disconnect between her title of manager and her actual work. On the flipside, I recently worked with a manager who was so laid back one wonders if his team understands that he isn't just a peer.

These are examples of what I've experienced many managers think are attributes for being a manager: either too strict and disconnected or too laid back. When I work with some managers, it seems they feel their role is to be overly harsh to make their point, or overly nice to make friends, hoping that one extreme or the other will garner results. Some are laser focused on numbers and reports to determine success, and may be unaware of how to set proper boundaries between getting along and getting things done. There is a separation when one goes from working alongside people to being responsible for the success of the department or company.

Without a focused effort from the organization to help effectively and positively deal with the identity of Manager, it becomes a challenge to determine which path to take. Individuals may gravitate toward the extremes of either harsh or lenient. There is a mental shift that many people in a management role are required to make so that they identify and are identified as being in charge. An additional challenge is that individuals who are handed a managerial role are rarely provided the holistic support and training to understand the depths of their role; as a result, gaps or disconnects with their team are inevitable.

People promoted to manager aren't taught to be managers in terms of leading people and team development. They are taught the technical requirements of executing tasks, which can create confusion when it comes to dealing with the people side of things. Speaking from direct experience, my manager training taught the technical elements of the organization only; I had to learn by trial and error ways to develop my team. When given an amount of control without the correlating parameters and having little to none of the proper soft-skills training for dealing with others, the interpretation of expectations is limited. This leads the manager to manage or control tasks, with a lack of awareness on how to motivate, encourage, and develop people.

Taking a closer look at this, many managers I work with want to do a good job and help the company succeed. At the same time, managers I have either worked for, worked with, or coached and trained became consumed by what is categorized as the tactical execution of day-to-day tasks, working to a number or the bottom line. Generally speaking, the skill set utilized is often that of telling, mainly because there is limited time, or the manager lacks the proper training to incorporate a more effective coaching approach of asking questions. This happens primarily because of the belief that it is his or her responsibility as a manager to take control and get results.

Having a reliable management team is important to organizations. Ideally, managers are point people as well as communication liaisons that navigate, understand, and accomplish the initiatives and directives of the company. These point people and communication liaisons execute tasks and identify how individuals perform based on objective, technical metrics. The conundrum is this: when people are underperforming, they are unsure of where to turn for help if their manager is more connected to the technical aspects instead of the people-related aspects. As a result, if the manager is one-dimensional and only fulfilling the definition of control, then he or she will likely be unavailable to support others to change behavior and/or improve. The call exists for training and coaching, either from completely different people or to develop these skills in the manager so that he or she can better provide for their team

Based on my experience, research, and findings in the field, the popular definition of the manager looks like this: primarily tactical, results-driven, report-oriented, and more closely aligned with the business entity itself rather than the people in it. The manager in our business world today leans toward utilizing people as a resource in creating and achieving success for the organization. As a result, the manager may be unaware how or unable to handle the human emotions of the team and instead rely on providing technical data to drive people forward. Since it takes more than facts and data for people to function and grow, who then develops the people?

THE TRAINER

When I think of a trainer what comes to mind is someone who possesses a level of knowledge or wisdom and who shares their knowledge through their teachings. They must be an expert at what they do, right? This is similar to saying the lead salesperson must be a good candidate for sales manager because they, of course, will also teach others how to sell well. Unfortunately, this is not a guarantee. As an example, I think back to my days as an equestrian. My trainer was very good at explaining how to carry myself, sit up, balance my weight, hold the reins in my hands, etc. On a horse he failed to reflect the same skills as those he verbalized. It begs the question, what makes a good trainer?

As a professional trainer, I am thankful that I know an extraordinary amount about the areas in which I train. Is the trainer an expert in their subject matter, or are they an expert in the skills of education? I think it is both. It takes being effective in both to see results. While I know a lot, there is more for me to know in my area of training.

Based on my work experience, training is being able to bring a new perspective to a topic, provide new information, and reframe it in a way for the student to create some sort of change. It requires patience and a methodology. A trainer is an educator. A trainer's goal is to provide information that enlightens the recipient. A trainer is most often a subject matter expert and skilled in dissecting a topic in order to help people see things in a new way.

In order to be a successful trainer and get results, I've learned there are several key ingredients for people to learn effectively:

awareness or the a-ha moment, information provided in a clear, structured, and organized way, a safe environment in which to model the new skill, an opportunity to practice, follow-up reinforcement, and confidence in the subject matter. It is the trainer's responsibility to create all of this in the training plan. These are certainly different considerations than the definition of the manager role I described earlier. To summarize, a successful trainer excels by applying a process for learning and connecting well with people.

There is more: if we consider that simply to change a habit requires time and repeated, deliberate effort, and that a goal of training is to encourage new behavior, then consequently, training too must require time and repetition. This is the reason it seems that companies which hire external trainers to come in for say a week, and then leave, see that the skills tend to have very little staying power. As a result, companies that spend resources on initiatives for training benefit greatly by having a long-term view and a priority on training. Speaking from personal experience, I see the most profound, positive outcomes on an initiative when I am able to partner with a client for several months, or years, at a time. Training a new skill, process, concept, etc. occurs with consistent reinforcement.

While the manager role lives more on the task side, the trainer role resides more on the people-focused side. It seems that the trainer and the reality of the manager are almost opposite in their roles. The way I've described them, the manager leans toward tasks and the company, and the trainer leans toward a process and the people they train. So where can they cross? Can the trainer live in the role of the manager?

Similar to a salesperson that is product-focused instead of client-centered, evidence from experience suggests the manager has the focus on the betterment of the organization while the trainer is consumed with the betterment of the student. Because the intent is different, I am simply pointing to the fact that if one is fulfilling the manager role as we have described then the role of trainer calls for a deliberate mental shift from wearing the manager's hat to the trainer's hat in order to share knowledge in an effective manner.

What keeps this from happening? It makes sense that if managers spend most of their time with staff, they also be the ones doing the training, correct? In reality, it is common for companies to either create a training department or continually access external resources to do the teaching. Sometimes this inadvertently enables managers to continue doing the telling rather than learning how to make the shift to trainer. As an example, our company had an opportunity to train managers how to coach. In so doing, we actually developed a training program that outlined first the differences between the coach and the manager, and second, provided a framework and process to implement a coaching meeting. This was a fascinating exercise because it added clarity around what I believe is happening time and again: people are given the controlling title of manager, and then, because of a lack of developmental programs at the managerial level, box themselves into the scenarios discussed earlier. By providing the managers with the tools to focus on their people, they became much more effective. Additionally, the benefit of understanding the trainer role may help a manager or coach better move past the challenges people face when learning something new. A methodical process focused on the student will in turn lead to growth. Of further note, the Association for Talent Development identifies coaching as a core competency for trainers to be successful in the classroom, thereby solidifying the call for coaching to be present in the training environment.

The Coach

When people are asked to think of their favorite coach, they have a tendency to think of sports they played, and then they choose the sports coach they worked with that made the biggest impression on them. It is interesting because we assign the label of coach related to who manages sports we play, and at the same time rarely do we say, "I worked for a manager at XYZ Company, and I think he was the best coach I ever had." It is even more surprising now considering that having a professional coach is increasingly popular. At the same time, it often seems we have a mental block that is preventing us from thinking of anyone who had a title other than a sports coach as being a big influence in our lives. This conundrum in and of itself is reason to look more deeply at what it means to be a coach.

A sports coach is, by universal understanding, a teacher who gives private or specialized training. There are a number of definitions that highlight that a coach is a trainer or instructor for an athlete and/or a sports team. Instead of looking at a label that is generally associated with who the sports coach coaches (i.e. an athlete), I want to look at the label in terms of the function of the role. In the definition cited above, the sports coach is an individual who gives private or specialized teaching. Based on this, a coach is associated with the general improvement of any one individual, regardless of area of focus, similar to a trainer. With that in mind the next question is, what makes a sports coach a coach and not a trainer? Also, can a coach be a manager or a trainer?

ICF defines coaching as partnering with clients in a thought-provoking and creative process that inspires them to maximize their personal and professional potential.

While a manager and a trainer typically possess in-depth knowledge about the matter at hand, the company's goals or the training topic, one of the most profound things I learned during coaching certification was this: instead of being about what you know and providing the right answer, it is about asking the right questions to help the other person discover their own answer. So this is the most glaring difference between a coach and a trainer, or a coach and a manager. A trainer figures out how to best transfer knowledge on their topic to the student. A manager identifies what they or the company wants done or changed, and then provides a directive. The coach, on the other hand, facilitates the expansion of self-awareness of the skills the student already possesses, provides an opportunity to explore possibilities and develop strategies, then supports planning and accountability.

The coach partners with the coachee to identify strengths, weaknesses, obstacles, how to overcome challenges, and ways to maximize potential. The coach may or may not know a lot about the topic at hand. We see that coaches we think of in the sports arena are experts at that sport. Alternatively, professional coaches are certified through a program approved or accredited by the International Coach Federation program and their primary responsibility is coaching competencies, processes, and methodologies. The function of the coach that I am referring to is partnering with the coachee to discover their own solutions. Speaking from experience, the role of the coach is the most challenging, and also the most liberating, compared to the manager or the trainer.

> *The coach may or may not know a lot about the topics at hand.*

Using an analogy, I like to think of a giant jigsaw puzzle. In very simple terms and based on the descriptions herein, the manager tells the individual to build the puzzle. The trainer shares how it should look when finished, then offers a way to go about putting it together. The coach asks questions so the individual or coachee identifies the pieces and evaluates the various ways it can be solved, and then empowers the coachee to solve in their own way and at their own pace.

As a coach, the primary methodology and biggest difference in the functional role versus the other two roles is powerful questions. Additionally, the coach listens actively and perceptively. This is part of what makes coaching so challenging because, based on behavioral science studies, listening and asking questions are two extremely challenging skills for most people to master. The coach's function is to partner in developing a roadmap through the use of questions and a dynamic ability to listen, and then tie themes and words together in the pursuit of growth for the coachee. As long as the goals of the coachee are ethical, it is to the role of the coach to empower the coachee to determine their own ultimate or correct solution. Projecting a solution or leading the coachee to a solution that is based on the coach's knowledge of the subject or preferences is considered training or managing.

If the primary function of the coach is to listen, ask, empower, encourage, motivate, and act as an accountability partner then on the flipside, can a manager encourage results through a coaching approach and likewise, the trainer teach based on the coaching philosophy? Yes.

> *... can a manager encourage results through a coaching approach and likewise, the trainer teach based on the coaching philosophy? Yes.*

Now What?

Each role has its strengths and focal points. How is it possible to optimize one's capabilities? What is the potential or benefit? If we are in any one of the three roles, where is it possible to cross over and utilize strengths of the others? Here are some next steps to help in that effort.

Let's start with a manager. If a manager wants to enhance his or her coaching and training skills, based on these definitions, then he or she can start by doing a few simple things:

1. Make time for each team member.
2. Ask before telling.
3. Make an effort to understand the long-term view of the individual team member.

4. Provide multiple ideas on how to achieve particular objectives and engage the individual to own follow-through.
5. Engage the team in the vision when beginning a new initiative.

As far as the trainer, what do they have to gain from the manager and coach? Some steps the trainer can take to capitalize on the strengths of the manager and coach:
1. Incorporate individual goals when training takes place.
2. Start with an agenda and plan, and then engage students early by asking for their expectations and objectives.
3. Use questions to set up concepts.
4. Use exercises that encourage group participation and small group discussion.
5. Set an expectation of what is to be accomplished and follow through.
6. Ask students how they will use what they learned.

Because the nature of the coaching relationship follows a strict set of core values and code of ethics, be cognizant of coaching parameters. There are several areas that add strength to the overall coaching experience to be gained by learning from the manager or trainer:
1. Understand the coachee's expected outcomes before the coaching relationship begins, and refer back to evaluate changes as well as accomplishments.

2. Establish a process to follow during coaching calls to provide structure. This may be as simple as asking, "to make best use of our time, where do you want to start the conversation?"
3. When opportunities to utilize personal experiences arise, or a subject presents itself in which the coach possesses a level of expertise, ask permission to brainstorm with the coachee ensuring the coachee is adding ideas and that the coach adds at least three ideas with zero investment in what the coachee decides.

FINAL WORDS

Getting back to incorporating my mom's advice on being well-rounded: so too can a manager, coach, and trainer become more well-rounded professionals by taking on new perspectives and expanding their skill sets. Most of us are in the business of developing people, so consistently developing ourselves makes sense. The International Coach Federation updated the Code of Ethics to include this as an ethical commitment.

Revisiting my teacher Mrs. Brown, based on what I know now, I recognize that she was so successful at deriving the best from us for the newspaper because she knew how to incorporate the strengths of all three roles. She gave us a task, took time to work with us to understand our thinking, offered both knowledge and suggestions when beneficial, and helped us find our own solutions. She had, either consciously or subconsciously, incorporated the various strengths of each role at the appropriate times to help us become a well-oiled, effective team.

Ultimately, all three professional roles work to bring about successful and productive individuals. Based on my experience teaching managers a coaching style, training professionals in a variety of programs, and being a coach to both managers and salespeople, I can say that there are clear results and growth when people are influenced by those that understand, adapt, and apply strengths from each of these roles. In my career I've seen the impact in results: everything from wholesalers I've trained and coached earning top awards among peers to a jump in revenue of 200% in 18 months, to a 50% earnings increase in less than three months.

People are set-up for experiencing incredible success when given the opportunity to work for and alongside people who can manage, train, and coach.

Kaleen is a managing partner with JAM Consulting Group. She is a professional coach, trainer, presenter, and program developer.

Clients appreciate that her passion for excellence and problem resolution has translated into being an effective partner on multiple levels and across an array of skill sets including communication, executive presence, and sales effectiveness.

Her experience the last 20 years stretches across management, sales, and relationship development. As a result, she possesses a truly client-centric approach and understanding of the complexities of relationships. Those elements, combined with her certified professional coaching designation, further differentiate her and the value that she brings to clients across the country.

Kaleen earned a B.S. in Marketing and graduated with Honors from Boston College in Chestnut Hill, MA.

www.linkedin.com/in/kaleenbarbera

COACHING FROM THE HEART
Betsy Laughter

REMEMBER THE REASONS YOU STARTED

Becoming a coach is a role many of us are led to after having life experiences that create within us both wisdom and a knowledge of how to approach transitions and challenges with ease and grace.

Seventeen years ago I walked across the stage to receive my degree, a bachelor's in Social Work, and I was ready to change the world. My ideas were so grand that I just knew I was going to single-handedly rid the world of poverty, sadness, and inequality. My first job was as a Social Worker / Discharge Planner on the Surgical and Cardiac floor at the very hospital where I was born. In my mind that was some great sign that I was destined to begin my journey for changing the world from the very place I began my life. It wasn't long before the beautiful rose colored glasses I was wearing began to lose their, let's say, rosiness. Red tape, laws, and insurance companies taught me how the corporate world plays a hand in ways our lives are affected when we seek help. Then there was the reality that not all people feel the same desire to make the world a better place. People struggle with addiction and histories of abuse, and some people have family members who want nothing to do with them, much less being willing to help take care of them after surgery. I continued my journey as a social worker through five more hospitals in five different cities. Along the way I earned my Master's degree in Social Work because it meant more money for me; let's be honest, even with a MSW social workers don't exactly rake in the mullah. As I started each new job in a new city I found hope that I was somehow finally going to make that grand breakthrough in the system and life was somehow going to be better for all of my patients. I was able to change my assigned population from Cardiac and Surgery patients to patients with Renal failure then on to Bone Marrow transplant then Intensive Care then Pediatrics, Pediatric Intensive care, Neonatal Intensive care and Mother/Baby. Each patient unit came with its own issues, its own red tape, and the thing I was feeling more and more was heart break. I met a patient who, after having a doctor repair the damage to his heart, continued to be abusive to his wife. I sat with women as they held their dying child. I worked with insurance companies to get a mother flown across the country so her children were able to learn how to care for her since she became paralyzed.

My career has been challenging and there have been days that the mere idea of meeting with yet another patient or family and finding a way to deal with their unplanned and undesired situation was almost more than I was ready to handle. Speaking of my personal life, wow, I hadn't imagined myself having some of those experiences. I came from a very loving and supportive family. I found myself in the midst of an abusive marriage that included my ex struggling with addiction. In the middle of that I was fired from a job and then had to move overnight because my then-husband gave me the ultimatum that I had to move or he was going without me. I had believed in fairytale endings so when I found myself in that reality it was absolutely one of the hardest things I ever faced. I eventually left that marriage, took the time to rebuild my life, and now I am remarried, have 2 beautiful children, and I am happy.

While I was able to change my personal situation I continued to deal with challenging and heart breaking situations at work, and I suddenly realized my heart wasn't really in it anymore. I was experiencing the thing they tell you about even in undergrad… burn out. My hope was there except reality was less than kind. I personally found myself at a crossroads. I chose to expand my expertise into coaching after suggestions from five different people in the course of one week.

The transition to coaching felt like a natural step for me because I have learned to lead with my heart. The challenge came with the business and marketing of coaching. Because these are increasingly important for coaches and outside my area of expertise, confusion set in. I found it appropriate to reset and return to the reasons I was led to coach in the first place.

Perhaps your experience is similar to mine. I have often been a sort of sounding board for the people I know because I had personal experiences in life that were challenging and heartbreaking. After struggling myself I chose to make my heartbreaking and sad experiences the foundation on which I built my own strength. This, in turn, created opportunities to use my personal experience for the benefit others. It was when I made the conscious decision to incorporate the lessons I learned from my own personal encounters into my work so that I was able to truly connect with my clients. This in turn helped me to establish trust and therefore helped clients work through life changing events and make challenging decisions.

Whatever you do in life there is a reason. Your reason is the heart of what you do and the driving force that will lead toward success. It is imperative we empower our true selves to spill in to our work. Inspirational quotes, positive language, and parables are great tools for ourselves and for coaching. It is the personal application combined with using them as coaches that will show clients we are being genuine in our work with them.

> *Inspirational quotes, positive language, and parables are great tools for ourselves and for coaching.*

Are You a Yoda?

My son has become a bit of a Star Wars fan. As cool as my son finds Darth Vader, I have been drawn to the ultimate coach and

Jedi Master, Yoda. Of all the quotes from the Star Wars movies, my favorite is from Yoda, "Do or do not. There is no try." This is deep and honest; it also takes a while to truly understand what it actually means. Let it sink in.

As a coach I want to challenge my clients to think in a positive way to promote equally positive change with a clear commitment.

> *... think in a positive way to promote equally positive change with a clear commitment.*

One of the coaching competencies is to use clear, direct language. Imagine having a conversation with someone and all they ever do is speak in what seems to be a riddle? As a coach I want to encourage my clients to think through their own situations and it is my job to help them move forward effectively. How can someone make progress if they remain stumped because they are lost in a riddle?

As you build rapport with your clients it is only fair that you communicate using clear, direct language. It is also appropriate that how you say what you say is positive and proactive because that is the best tool to create positive thoughts. A challenge that arises here is when a client is explaining a past experience or is negative. On the one hand, giving our clients the space to be themselves is important. On the other hand, coaching competencies tell us that a focus on the past is mental health instead of coaching. A focus on the negative reinforces the negative. Especially initially, it is important to discover the balance between coaching ethically which means focusing forward and also giving the client time to share their story. In the International Coach Federation (ICF) Competencies Level Table, which explains how coaching competencies are evaluated, it says an applicant will not pass in the area of Ethics and Standards if, "The conversation is based primarily in the past, particularly the emotional past (therapeutic mode)." Under questions it also says a coach will not pass in the area of Powerful Questioning if, "Coach frequently asks informational questions or questions that keep the client in the past or in present detail of a situation rather than in forward thinking."

What does this mean for coaches? It means that when starting with a new client some sharing of their history makes sense as long as the purpose is getting to know the client and understanding where they are at now. It means that sometimes a few minutes on a story or to vent are helpful to the client, and then the coach partners with the client to move forward.

As the rapport strengthens, determine the best time to hold up the proverbial mirror for your client to see themselves in a different way. This is when I choose to challenge their self-talk and show them how when they choose words that are positive, especially when referring to themselves, it affects their thought process and eventually their approach towards their goals.

A recent client of mine is at an age that she is unsure of the path she wants to take right now. Our biggest challenge initially was helping her see and hear that her language allowed little room for owning her own life. When I asked her what she desired for her life she was quick to tell me what her parents and her grandmother wanted for her instead. I then challenged her to exchange the language of what her family wants for her to language that defines the desires and goals she has for herself. By giving her space to express it her own way initially, I was able to gain insight on where she is in her life. Accept your clients as they are in the moment. Start where they are, begin the process of establishing trust, and pave a path for progress.

Let's look further into the way we communicate with our clients and how important it is to be authentic. I referred to Yoda earlier and how his inspirational quotes make complete sense after some time for the words and their meaning to sink in. I love a wordsmith as much as anyone, and there is a time and place for that. Our communication with clients, instead of being a riddle that has to be sorted out, is intended to be clear and direct. Life has its own set of challenges and there is more room for growth during a coaching session when we communicate clearly and directly.

Using positive language is a reflection of your belief in your client and the forward focus of coaching. In other words, be positive and use positive, forward thinking language.

Encourage and support clients to be themselves and embrace what makes them unique. As coaches, walk the talk and do the same; be authentic. As we continue to learn and evolve, and as we focus forward and are proactive, our language will evolve along with our experiences.

SHARE YOUR STORY (SORT OF)

For years as a Social Worker I found myself feeling challenged to establish trust and respect from the patients I was working with because I had been taught in both in undergrad and grad school that revealing anything personal with my patients was unprofessional. I struggled with this idea that I was expected to guide people through life changing decisions without telling them my story so they feel connected to me, and without the knowledge that I actually identified with the struggle they were experiencing at that moment. It was years before I took ownership of my interactions with my clients, and once I did allow myself some professional freedom and began to appropriately share some of my own personal experiences with patients and their families, I began to notice a complete change in the interactions and outcomes of our interactions. It is possible to have empathy for a client without making it all about you when sharing personal information. It means developing within yourself the ability to connect with your client, to place yourself in their shoes, to understand how they may be feeling, where their frustrations are coming from, and being able to see the big picture at the same time. I learned how to step outside of the box appropriately and be personal in my practice. This idea of sharing a bit of my own personal experience with clients has transitioned into my role as a coach, and I believe it has made all the difference.

When a client is sharing something deeply personal or facing a major challenge, if it helps the client to know you really do understand, asking permission to share a personal experience can make sense. Additionally, if a client is stuck, sharing multiple ideas and including personal experience can also be helpful when handled appropriately. As a coach, know that personal sharing is for the benefit of the client, gain permission first, and be open to any or all possible reactions from the client.

> *As a coach, know that personal sharing is for the benefit of the client, gain permission first, and be open to any or all possible reactions from the client.*

BE TRUE TO YOU

In the last year or so it seems the new catch phrase or hot word is to be authentic. It is a trendy word right now and it is vital in coaching. If you represent yourself in a way that fails to reflect who you truly are, people will eventually be able to tell and your artificial persona will be unable to keep up with the charade.

Several years ago I had an epiphany about myself and my personal gifts or talents. The very thing that has become one of my most valuable strengths was initially something I thought was negative. I am rather emotional and sensitive. In fact, I am the poster child for the adage "wear your emotions on your sleeve". I mentioned earlier about how I learned to channel my own personal tragedies into strengths, and this is also another strength I have stumbled upon. As a child I remember being told things like, "you are so emotional" or "you are too sensitive" or "you are so dramatic". Until a few years ago I saw these as faults. Then, at some point, I realized that my personality is such that I am able to connect with people who are experiencing personal crisis which in turn empowers me to build trust and rapport rather quickly. This in turn helps me to be more successful working with my clients. That very ability to connect with people stems from my sensitivity and wearing emotions on my sleeve. I have learned that wearing my emotions on my sleeve is actually one of my personal gifts and part of what makes me unique.

So as a coach I encourage you to identify the personality traits you possess that will make you stronger in your practice. We all have weaknesses and things to improve upon; if we spend all our time focusing what appears to be a weakness we can become paralyzed. Instead, if we identify our strengths and use those as a foundation to build upon, we have something to start with and a powerful set of tools.

> *... if we identify our strengths and use those as a foundation to build upon, we have something to start with and a powerful set of tools.*

In addition to owning who you are and identifying your strengths, I think it is equally important to utilize tools and exercises in your coaching that reflect you authentically. As I began my practice I found myself wanting to do things exactly like I was taught during the process of my certification. Certification programs that are approved or accredited by the ICF have very strict guidelines on what coaching is, how it works, and the competencies of a coach. Participating in coaching certification calls for being open to learning a different profession and processes. The challenge for me was that it is very different from what I normally do as a mental health professional, so that reflected into my practice. This struggle created a delay in my ability to effectively develop rapport and trust with my clients. It is essential to differentiate my roles and recognize what coaching is and is not. According to the ICF Code of Ethics, coaching is focused forward. As a mental health professional we often spend time discussing the past. Since my focus as a coach is to help my clients create goals and plans for themselves, it is essential that I be clear on my role with the client and on what that means.

It is my opinion that we can learn a great deal from other coaches and also from mental health professionals. Ultimately it is our responsibility to take what we learn and make it our own as long as we are in keeping with the ethics for the profession. Once I took ownership of my approach, when using the tools and exercises I incorporate into my work with clients I felt more confident, more myself, and I have an increased sense of ownership of my practice.

FIND YOUR PASSION

I enjoy working with people in transition. More specifically I prefer to work with women in transition. I like working with people who are interested in making changes in a holistic approach to their lives. In other words, they are focused on their personal and professional life, their relationships with people, and the roles they play. I also prefer to work with people who want balance. What this translates to for me is that I am less comfortable working with people who only focus on their professional lives and the volume of work they handle. I am not in that place of my life and to offer coaching to someone I have trouble understanding and connecting with is unfair.

Think of it like eating ice cream. When you choose your favorite flavor you enjoy the entire experience, savoring the flavor, and you eat every bite. If you go with a flavor that isn't your favorite, you find yourself wishing that you had gotten your favorite anyway so you fail to enjoy it as much.

Without passion and focus as a coach, you may find yourself working with clients that you struggle to build rapport with so in turn, their likelihood of having a positive experience is reduced. I encourage people to find a coach they are comfortable with and trust. I think as coaches we have the same responsibility to be selective of the clients we agree to work with to ensure we offer our best and help them reach their desired outcome.

THE HEART WANTS WHAT THE HEART WANTS

Being a coach can be incredibly rewarding and for some quite lucrative. In order to build a successful coaching business there are many things to consider. Prices, marketing, networking options, whether you coach in person or via phone or skype, your budget, your workspace, and so forth. All of those are important for the business to run smoothly. It is also imperative to stay connected with the reason you chose this path in the first place. Reasons for continuing may change over time; the passion will generally stay the same.

In addition to your passion, I encourage you to stay true yourself and what makes you unique. We, as coaches, all possess some characteristic that gives us the ability to work with clients and help them to create, plan for, and achieve their goals. We are all different and equal and are effective working with clients in different ways as long as we are true to who we are as individuals. Being able to incorporate our true personalities into our work will lead to our clients feeling we are being authentic in our work with them, and in turn will help to build trust so they work toward their goals freely.

Remember that as coaches we are unique. We each offer our own unique value by finding our niche and being self-aware of who we work with best. This will lead to better outcomes for clients and a higher sense of satisfaction for us in our work.

> *... as coaches we are unique.*
> *We each offer our own unique value by finding our niche and being self-aware of who we work with best.*

All of these factors are part of what helps us to be true to the heart of what we do as coaches. Being true to yourself leads to personal satisfaction which empowers you to be confident, leading to you being a coach who truly makes a difference. We've heard the cliché about loving what you do… this is true and it also supports the idea that once we find our natural gifts and passions then we succeed as we are meant to in this world.

WHAT DOES YOUR HEART WANT?

Given that coaching is a totally unique profession and calls for a different approach and way of thinking than other professions, how do you discover what your heart wants?

I encourage my clients to take some time alone, get quiet, and go back to a time in their lives when they felt completely authentic. It is in those moments that our true, unique gifts are surfacing. By getting quiet and focusing on the very things that make us happy we rediscover our passions and gifts. I guide clients to be specific. Think of your favorite colors, your favorite song, your favorite shirt, what makes you laugh, your best memory; get in there and focus on all your senses. Write it all down and then tell yourself the story of that person, who he/she is, and what is significant about his/her story. I partner with my clients to find something tangible that is a reminder of the experiences to serve as a solid reminder in their journey towards finding their true gifts and passion. This is the same for me as a coach and how I have learned to coach from the heart.

When I did this exercise myself I was taken back to my childhood and remembered how I was the first to save a stray animal and also take it home, feed it, and perhaps I even went as far as to use every blanket my mother owned to make a bed for homeless creatures. That memory then took me to the days when I was a teenager and spent hours talking with my friends who had broken hearts from young love. I made it my mission to be their support and confidant, and I remember how valued I felt in those moments. I also remembered how bright pinks, greens, yellows, and blues help me to feel alive and powerful. I feel most alive and myself when I am present with other people and helping them to find solutions to their challenges. There is a picture of me as a little girl that I keep as a reminder of my passion and gifts. I was probably 8 years old, in the back yard, wearing shorts and a pink t-shirt. My hair is in a side ponytail and I am dancing. For someone else to see it they may only see the picture as I described it; for me I see the young girl who is full of life, confident, and open to the world; she is compassionate and ready to help anyone. That picture is my tangible reminder that as a coach, as long as I give from my heart, work with clients in the best way that I can, and utilize approaches and exercises that work with my personality and fit with my personal value system, then I will be assured to give my personal and professional best because I coach from the heart.

I encourage you to reflect on who you truly are as a person and as a coach. Own your passion and gifts, and you will be an amazing coach to those who will benefit the most.

Betsy Laughter is a Certified Professional Coach. She is passionate about working with people in personal and professional transitions.

Betsy believes each person is born with their own unique gifts. She enjoys working with clients to reconnect with their gifts and to figure out how to incorporate those gifts into their everyday lives while living with more passion and satisfaction.

Betsy has spent the last 17 years working as a medical Social Worker and she is proud of her ability to connect with people and their family members who are in crisis or a major life transition. She thrives on helping them determine what options and possible solutions are available and then further working to navigate through the process of change.

www.linkedin.com/in/betsy-laughter

COACHING: THE TOTAL PACKAGE
Jennifer Maxwell Parkinson

Coaching and image consulting work together, hand-in-hand, to aid individuals in aligning their inner and outer messaging to themselves and the outside world. By doing this, they are better able to access and utilize a variety of tools to project their true, authentic selves in every aspect of their lives.

> *Coaching and image consulting work together, hand-in-hand, to aid individuals in aligning their inner and outer messaging to themselves and the outside world.*

Our inner and outer vision of ourselves develops at a very young age. We can be easily influenced and, for the most part, are programmed to accept the information we receive from elders, authorities, and loved ones. The messages that have been projected on us and that we ourselves have perpetuated then create our image. Whether the messages are from parents, grandparents, teachers, siblings, friends, or a combination of all these people in our lives, we trust that their intentions were good.

As coaches we can see in our clients, and with less ease in ourselves, that as adults many of us are living with conflicting inner and outer messaging. There comes a time when we are well served to step up and out, into a self of our own intentional creation, and find our harmony between our inner self and our outer self.

As a coach we listen and ask questions, guiding the client through a deeper thought process than they may naturally engage in on their own. As an image consultant, we take on the role of consultant with coaching skills enhancing our services. As a coach we empower the client to arrive at an actionable task or solution. As an image consultant we make concrete suggestions for the client. As an image expert, we have access to knowledge and information that is new for the client. It becomes incumbent upon us to make suggestions in addition to partnering with the client through parts of the process. In both cases, we guide our clients through the process.

In order to successfully blend the two very different roles, we learn a dance that pushes us to the edge while staying within the line. This process includes discussing potential goals with a client. If the goal is a better job, their personal presentation becomes one of the topics for review and assessment. In image consulting this happens through a series of personal exercises such as picking out the five outfits that make them feel most professional, then discussing when and in what situation these outfits are worn, plus what exactly motivated the positive feeling.

Changing one's image inside and out has a huge effect on self-esteem and self-confidence. When a person can actually see, in the mirror or in their mind's eye, his or her own life including who they are and who they want to be, it aids them in truly focusing and developing a clear path to follow.

A fine line to be aware of and respect is the line between coach and therapist. A therapist is trained to assess, diagnose, determine direction, and give advice. What does crossing that line mean? Focusing on the past or problems, or telling the client to handle a personal situation in a specific way. Instead, coaches focus on empowering the client to move forward and image consultants focus on supporting how the client portrays themselves.

There are times when a conversation about personal goals will lead to a wardrobe makeover, or an office or home renovation. The ultimate goal is to support the client in going from where they are today to being their very best in every possible way.

When I first meet with a client, we decide together if I will employ both image consulting and coaching methodologies, or just one or the other. Many times, a client will start out working on their image and as we talk about what brought them to their goals, they discover that it will be beneficial to combine image consulting and coaching. When asking questions about their life, goals, likes and dislikes, oftentimes the client will discover that thinking through these questions is a new experience. Sometimes I will have a client who begins with just the image aspects and later discovers that they want to continue on with the coaching. Sometimes, I will work either solely as an image consultant or solely as a coach. Most of my clients prefer both.

Note: The following stories are fictional while drawing on multiple experiences; the stories in this chapter are included to help the reader understand how to work with the total person.

MARY - WHO AM I NOW?

For some clients, life is turned upside down in an instant. Mary was preparing for her 37th birthday when she received a shocking diagnosis of breast cancer. Fortunately, it was caught early. At the same time, life as she knew it was now changed. The road to becoming cancer-free was, on one hand, long, hard, exhausting, and scary. On the other hand, it was successful, hopeful, and initiated a welcome and valuable rebirth.

After completing the process of treatment, Mary found herself on the other side of a life she no longer recognized. Nothing about her once-so-perfect life made sense. She was changed. Mary made a conscious decision to give herself the gift of a new chapter, a new way of being, plus an image consultant and a coach to guide her on this journey into her next birthday and beyond.

Pre-cancer diagnosis Mary found great joy and satisfaction in her work as a psychologist; afterwards it changed. When Mary learned about her illness, she immediately re-focused her entire life on the mission of getting well. She referred many of her patients to other psychologists and lightened her daily load. She analyzed her diet and realized there were many changes to be made. She researched, extensively, every morsel of food she ate and how it impacted or nourished her body. She realized that a truly health-focused diet required 100% organic products and far more greens than she normally consumed. The race was on. Time was of the essence. She was willing to do whatever it took. She began eating new varieties and combinations of foods, and even planting her own garden and growing her own vegetables and herbs to ensure the purity and quality of everything she ate. Rather than feeling horrified, Mary became a student with a refreshed interest in her future.

We talked about Mary's life as it had been before for a shared baseline awareness. Then we talked for hours about how she viewed her future. As a consultant I asked her to keep a journal each day. The amount she wrote varied; each week we agreed on a different topic for her to write about. One week it was all the new foods she was discovering and how she felt after each meal. Another week was focused on her body and movement. Another on the people she was spending time with and how they made her feel. She also kept track of where she went, what she wore, and how she felt.

Mary was paying a new level of attention to her personal sense of completeness, just as she was her diet. In addition to eliminating artificial foods and chemical toxins, Mary decided to eliminate toxic people, those who showed themselves as less than true friends, or who were unable to be around her during her struggles.

This was a new time for Mary. She came to realize that while she loved the outdoors, she spent little time away from her office. She had once been a decent athlete and then she had stopped participating in sports in order to accommodate a hectic patient schedule. She decided it was time for all of this to change. She took time to re-focus on the activities that gave her joy. She purged many of the possessions that she once held so dear. She began to prioritize the experiences that she wanted to have in her life now. She started walking outdoors every day and she began to do a short yoga session each morning and evening.

Mary had a small circle of close friends with whom she spent time cooking, listening to music, and exploring the world. They were the keepers. These people and experiences were the priorities in Mary's new life. Now, she had space to welcome a wonderful man and a beautiful relationship for the future. Mary had many opportunities to recreate her life and she was ready to do it. She was forty years old, healthy, and preparing to live a long life. She was unsure what to do with her life.

For Mary the woman staring back at her in the mirror was someone different. Before the cancer, Mary's hair had been straight, long, and brown. After the cancer it had grown back grey and curly. Who was that old woman looking back at her now? Her new goal was to find the beautiful woman within. A new feminine beauty was born and Mary wanted to meet her and live into her. She wanted an introduction to Mary 2.0.

Who was Mary now? She knew she enjoyed helping people. With the knowledge she had acquired during her illness, she realized one option was to help others by writing a cookbook and teaching classes about the new lifestyle practices that helped her get healthy and strong. Whenever she entertained, her friends raved about the meals she prepared. She approached a friend who owned a restaurant to share her new-found passion for healthful eating. The friend hired Mary to teach classes and cook a new healthy menu for the restaurant. Slowly, Mary started seeing and feeling the person she wanted to be; the new Mary was emerging. The missing link was a new personal style or look to present her to the world.

Mary had been fairly simple in her style. She purchased garments she thought covered her body and looked good enough. She rarely took risks or felt the desire to experiment with new looks. She soon discovered that just as she had been creative in her cooking and lifestyle changes, she had the ability to reflect that in her appearance. I assigned her an exercise to go through catalogues and find pictures that struck a chord with her. With her new curly hair and boyish frame, Mary wanted to find a way to feel more feminine. We went shopping. With my guidance as her image consultant, she tried on clothing that was different than before. The point was to go shopping to find her new personal style. Through this exercise she discovered that flowing soft fabrics over a foundation of lacy lingerie made her feel beautiful and sexy. The feel and fit of her clothes combined with soft, feminine colors became important for the first time in Mary's life. She discovered a new value for her life and her feminine self in her life. Given this opportunity, Mary created a look, a home, and a life that she loved and that loved her back. Mary continues to find excitement in all aspects of growth in her life and is still, happily, cancer-free.

LEARNING POINTS FROM WORKING WITH MARY

As an image consultant with people like Mary, I talk about their internal image as well as their external appearance. We discuss who they want to be and how they want to express that in their appearance. When we shop I point out clothing and fabrics that fit their new desired self.

As a coach with people like Mary, I listen deeply to what they say and also what they do not say. I ask them questions about what impacts their choices, their values, and their priorities. I ask them to define goals and plan strategies for change.

What I learned from working with clients like Mary is that when people make their own choices and want to change, their progress is rapid and their success is both powerful and meaningful.

> *... when people make their own choices and want to change, their progress is rapid and their success is both powerful and meaningful.*

MARK - AM I INVISIBLE?

Mark had held the same position in a financial planning firm for a few years and was repeatedly passed over for promotions. An opening for his same position was available in a different location. Mark requested a transfer thinking of it as a nice change and a way to bring him closer to family there. This move was a lateral move and not considered a promotion. Human Resources had told Mark that the move required him to make significant changes to both his image and his management style.

We met at my office. His company had sent him to me for an overhaul. They asked me to help Mark pinpoint what it was that was holding him back from moving up in the company. His new boss saw his potential and wanted to support him.

Mark arrived wearing a conservative grey suit, a traditional button down oxford shirt, striped tie, and black wing tip shoes. His hair was long, fuzzy, thinning, and mostly grey. He immediately shared with me that he was unable to understand the reasons, after spending a fortune on new suits, no one seemed to notice or treat him differently or with respect.

I asked him how he wanted to see his life change. He told me that while he liked his job, and felt he was good at it, he was frustrated and felt that his peers in the office barely spoke to him about anything other than work. People stood at his office door to talk to him, rarely entering. Previously his office had a revolving door of visitors. In looking back, he realized his coworkers and staff were coming in to shoot the breeze, not to report to him or seek his professional support.

We began exactly where his day began, in his new office. Mark was told to take his management position in the new location more seriously. In an effort to oblige, he decorated his office with a large plant near the door. He thought it added warmth to the stark space. Unfortunately, upon my entering it became clear that the plant was more of a barrier, almost a wall, stopping people from entering his office. It had to move. We added a few pictures of family, books, office appropriate items, and some inspirational messages on the walls to create a much more welcoming, positive environment. As a finishing touch to show Mark was thinking ahead, making changes to his management style, and supporting his team he put up a small chalk board to broadcast a new team goal each week. It was intended to generate conversation and team connection; it did.

Outside of work Mark was happily married and, together with his wife, busily making new friends across a variety of shared interests. Through our discussions, Mark came to understand that he wanted to align his social personality style with his work personality.

Previously Mark had been considered a hip dresser. His style was very casual with bright ties and short sleeve shirts. We soon discovered that when Mark put on his Brooks Brothers suit it was not because it represented him and his style. It was because he believed that was how a professional dressed. He had put his own distinct personal style away in favor of the role he was playing. Mark wanted to learn how to have fun with his wardrobe in his new position, to make it personal and still appropriate in his new surroundings.

Mark loved fun patterns and colors so he decided to express this in his boxer shorts and socks. That way he felt he looked good all under. He also became more creative in his ties, using colors and patterns that were made of quality silk and knotted to perfection. Suits fit him well so he found interesting, subtle patterns. He also shaved his head to a very short style, taking 20 years off his appearance. Mark had gone from hipster to stuffy and then, ultimately, downshifted that stuffiness into a top tier executive embracing his own unique style. As Mark quickly learned, when you dress the part and know your true goals, you align to become the person you set out to be.

He was nervous about people noticing his dramatic change of style and was pleasantly surprised to find his coworkers were immediately more open and receptive to him. He became more visible in a positive, upbeat way. He was noticed in the best light possible - for his hard work. When he dressed in clothing that was more creative, aligned with his true self, and still perfectly professional, Mark was able to excel at his job while feeling authentic, aligned, and comfortable. He was promoted three times the following year.

LEARNING POINTS FROM WORKING WITH MARK

As an image consultant I talk with people like Mark about what does or does not work in attire based on their profession and geographical area. Often times clients think a stereo-typical style is best when in reality it is their own style expressed appropriately that works best.

As a coach I listen as clients like Mark explore what they really want, what really matters to them, and how they want to create their ideal. Then I ask questions so they identify their barriers and plan their action steps.

What I learn from working with people like Mark is to have fun because it truly empowers them to be their own best self which in turn is the foundation for their success.

CATHERINE - WHERE DO I GO FROM HERE?

Catherine was a mother of two small children when her husband left her for a younger woman. She was in shock. She realized it was up to her to start her life over and somehow take care of her family. She came to me for guidance in helping her recreate her life as a single mother.

Through our conversations and exercises I learned she was emotionally drained to her core, causing her self-esteem to go into hiding. While married, she had been a full-time mom who spent her days doting on her children, caring for her home, socializing with friends, and with her husband. She had only really worked inside of her home because she married as soon as she graduated high school.

Her husband left her and her children with no money and no place to live so she and her children were living with her parents. In order to pay the bills, she started cleaning houses. Her new uniform was leggings, a tee shirt, hair in a ponytail, and no make-up. When she was married she had enjoyed styling her hair, applying different skin care serums and make-up, and dressing in jeans and nice tee shirts. Her recent turn of events meant she unable to invest the same energy in her appearance as before.

When we began working together, she was devastated and unable to imagine how to live without her husband. She was on a very limited budget. She knew that she wanted to create a new life for herself and her children. She also knew she wanted to change how she looked and felt.

Through conversations we talked about how to be aware of circumstances, self, and opportunities. Catherine wrote a list of things she liked to do, her strengths, what kind of life she saw for her future, and what habits or behaviors might hold her back.

She enjoyed watching courtroom dramas and had good listening skills along with being detail-oriented. She also had great writing, typing, and speaking abilities. Her self-esteem and emotional frustration were the things she felt were holding her back. By combining her skills, talents, and pleasures, she determined that she wanted to become a court reporter.

Reaching this goal meant going back to school. I worked with her to create a strategy. Catherine called a variety of local colleges in search of job openings. She knew that universities and colleges often offered reduced tuition to employees. She was ecstatic to get a job as a receptionist at a community college.

Together we created a three-year plan to get her through school and into her next job. Once she actually saw her new life as a bright light in front of her she felt better about her new direction. She reinvented the person she had been into the empowered, self-directed woman she was becoming.

As important as her internal goals were, syncing her outer image to reflect her new goals supported being her best self. We did a series of exercises illustrating what she saw in the mirror and what she dreamed of seeing. She said she liked simple, easy to wear, tailored clothing. She wanted to fit in, look pulled together, and be coordinated.

Given her limited funds we shopped at consignment stores for a basic core wardrobe for Catherine to mix and match for work, school, and mom-time. Catherine had been great at editing her own drawers and closets. She decided to offer to help a number of her friends do the same in exchange for some of their clothing and accessories. She had her hair cut into an easy care style and bought some basic drugstore make-up.

When she saw her new look and clearly saw the possibility of her goals in her view, she realized she was over the fear of being alone. The next time she saw her ex-husband, a year later, she realized that she was now a completely different person from the girl he had married. The benefits of the coaching and lifestyle changes she made moved her beyond her anger and her sadness by helping her focus on her future self.

When her family and friends saw Catherine's new look, her fresh focus, and the happiness emanating from her, they were thrilled. Her confidence level continued to strengthen as she moved closer to her goals. Through our work together, she created a structure in her life for both herself and her children. She shared that once she secured a solid job she was going to set aside money each month to move with her children into a home of their own. Catherine now works as a paralegal and is happily remarried.

LEARNING POINTS FROM WORKING WITH CATHERINE

As an image consultant I work with people like Catherine to develop a functional look that feels good and serves them professionally too. I also work with them based on their budget.

As a coach I work with people like Catherine to focus forward to create the life and style they want.

By working with people like Catherine I have learned how important focusing on the future and possibilities is for confidence. In turn confidence supports taking action and moving forward.

> *... how important focusing on the future and possibilities is for confidence. In turn confidence supports taking action and moving forward.*

COACHING AND IMAGE CONSULTING

Coaching can manifest itself in many forms. Professional coaches are trained and so have knowledge of certain industry and training guidelines. At the same time, we all coach in our own personal way: I began my career as an image coach. As my business evolved, I added professional and life coaching to provide a more well-rounded, complete service.

As you can see from the examples in this chapter, each client is unique and has their own objectives, goals, and dreams. A dream becomes a reality when it is clearly defined as a goal with steady, achievable steps that can be taken each day to move closer to the pinnacle envisioned.

If you wish to combine image and life coaching, it is just as important to study the image aspect as it is the coaching with a well-respected institution. Knowing about style, body types, fabrics, colors, expectations, products, wardrobes, etiquette, and personal comfort with appearance is foundational to image consulting. Being a great listener and friend gives you a passion for coaching; training provides the foundational ability to coach and a clear system or method to be a professional.

There are many dimensions that go into coaching the total person: the core competencies of a coach, the coaching Code of Ethics, techniques of coaching, knowing how to ask coaching questions, and a clear system. All of this and more helps you help clients define their goals to create change and this often includes the way they present themselves to the world. In some cases, this extends beyond appearance to working with their communication skills and styles, body language, and etiquette.

> *There are many dimensions that go into coaching the total person: the core competencies of a coach, the coaching Code of Ethics, techniques of coaching, knowing how to ask coaching questions, and a clear system.*

It is a privilege to be entrusted to do this work. There is incredible satisfaction in knowing that you have taken the time to become an expert in the areas that impact individuals on a deep, life-altering level. I wish you the best.

Jennifer Maxwell Parkinson is an Image Expert, Speaker, and a Certified Professional Coach with the Center for Coaching Certification.

As founding president of the Association of Image Consultants International and president of LOOK Consulting International, Ms. Parkinson served as a national spokesperson for the Image Industry. Jennifer has been featured as a recognized expert in numerous publications including The New York Times, Forbes, Newsweek, Vogue, and Men's Health. She has been featured on both TV and radio and is a contributing author to "Fit and Fabulous at 40 Plus" published by Prevention magazine for the chapter on body image.

Ms. Parkinson helps her clients create their vision and translate it into reality. Jennifer works with both individual and corporate clients who seek to maximize their personal and business effectiveness through personal and executive style, public relations, team building, and customer service best practices. Some of her clients include AT&T, Condé Nast, Saks Fifth Avenue, Corcoran Group and The United Nations.

www.jenniferparkinson.com

MAPPING YOUR DREAM
Shaddae Renee

For many people, the beginning stages of a dream are often filled with excitement and hope. Thoughts of possibilities cause their hearts to race as they experience the thrill. They experience bursts of energy and sleepless nights because their minds are racing. With new found courage they are ready to take on the world. Life is wonderful and inviting. They feel and believe that their dream will come true.

Sometimes, as time passes, fear kicks in, and then they realize that they have wandered into the unknown. Questions fly and there is heightened uncertainty whether the dream will come true. They may be tempted to let go. As time goes on they attempt to settle into the daily routine, and still the dream lingers. They begin to tell themselves that they were being irrational and that someone else is better suited to bring the dream to reality. They begin to feel insecure. They push the dream behind all of the daily errands and concerns, giving less and less thought to it. Eventually, the dream becomes a distant memory. They become passive about life, taking things as they happen. They choose to remain in their comfort zone living vicariously through others.

Then, as more time passes, their comfort zone no longer satisfies them. They know deep within that there is more that can be achieved and experienced. Periodically they wonder, what if I pursued my dream? Can it become a reality?

Dreams, by nature, are abstract and intangible. They become material when you assign tangible attributes to them. Dreams are attainable when the underlying goals are actionable, clearly defined, properly measured, and consistently monitored.

There are different types of dreams: Time Sensitive dreams, Skill or Talent-Bound dreams, and Flexible dreams. Time Sensitive dreams require action at specified times for them to take formation. Skill or Talent-Bound Dreams require certain attributes of the dreamer that may come naturally or with practice. For Skill or Talent-Bound dreams without timeframes it is crucial to leverage strengths and supplement any weaknesses. Flexible dreams are dreams that can be accomplished at any age and the requirements to obtain them can be met by anyone that demonstrates courage, desire, and perseverance. Within the Flexible dream there will be timeframes as well as skills and talents that are preferable; the dream itself will still be achievable if a specific deadline is missed or if there is a lack of a particular skill. A Flexible Dream can be reconstructed and will change as time and circumstances change.

The purpose of this chapter is to guide you through the process of achieving your dream by creating goal maps. There are

three steps:
1. Visualizing the Dream and Identifying Obstacles
2. Moving the Dream into Actionable Steps
3. Leveraging Resources

1. VISUALIZING THE DREAM AND IDENTIFYING OBSTACLES

When you visualize your dream completely, including all the senses, it is more real. Often during the process obstacles come to mind so writing them down and then planning how to address them prepares you to make your dream a reality.

Take a moment to clear your mind. Think of something that you want to acquire or desire to do in your life. Now explore what your life will be like when you make it happen. Where are you? What do your surroundings look like? What do you hear? What do you feel? What do you taste? What do you smell? Who is with you? All of these questions will help you to gain a complete sensory picture of what it will be like living within the existence of your dream.

Now take your dream and your answers to the above questions and write them down. An important part of visualizing your dream is to keep a record. In the beginning stages, your ideas and pictures are filled with great detail and imagery. Harness this stage by journaling or keeping a log of notes that you can reference in the future. You will want this information as you follow the process.

Next ask yourself and write: What do I want? and What do I require? Align every defined step and goal with the answers to these questions. The things you want are aspects of your dream that can be adjusted. Your requirements are the elements it will take to realize your dream. For example, if you require a certain level of income to maintain your daily life, tailor your dream to ensure the requirement is met.

SETBACKS

Setbacks can be financial, emotional, physical, mental, or social. At times setbacks create a domino effect, affecting multiple areas at once. Many setbacks are temporary circumstances. The principle to keep in mind when facing a setback is patience. Focus your attention on navigating through, and then revisit your prior plan and objectives. Take time to identify your new steps, resources, timeframes, and objectives so you redefine your plan and actions.

Once the plan is redefined, take action. Rebuild your motivation and refocus on consistency. Setbacks only thwart a plan if there is inaction. In the initial phases of goal mapping, there is a time where brainstorming is performed to identify what-if scenarios. This is a preventative tactic to prepare for potential threats to the plan. At this stage, there are courses of action that are identified in the event the what-if scenario occurs. These actions can be employed quickly and will likely reduce the amount of time it takes to resolve a setback, and also lessen its impact on the plan. Be creative, flexible, and open-minded. A new route may become available for obtaining the goal.

> *Be creative, flexible, and open-minded.*

FACING FEAR AND FAILURE

Dreams may be discouraged by fear or by failure. Fear is an experience whereby a person envisions a future event, anticipates a negative outcome, and makes a decision based on that imagined negative outcome. Choosing to act even though you may have some fear is a crucial step in achieving your dream. You may fail or fall short in the process of achieving your goals. Acknowledging this helps alleviate some of the reluctance to take a chance and step out in faith. Productive actions will move you forward. Adopting the mindset of a student will help you find the lesson in each experience so that you can apply it to the next step. Failure is just a checkpoint and an opportunity to adjust the process. Persevere and leverage your resources. There are people who have walked similar paths and may have feedback or advice that will help.

At the end of each day, take time to reflect on the challenges and the positive occurrences. What were some of your accomplishments of the day? Write them down so you can revisit them later when you want encouragement.

CREATE POSITIVE BELIEFS

Identify fears or negative beliefs and then write down a statement that challenges that belief. For example: Negative Statement: "I will not be able to go back to school and obtain the degree." Challenge Statements: "I will find a school that offers the program and schedule flexibility that works best for my life. I will research financial aid options and create a financial plan to pay for tuition. I will seek advice from counselors and support from family and friends. I will obtain the degree."

Challenge statements are effective in preventing the progression of a negative belief and assist in the creation of positive thoughts, which help open the mind to alternatives. Through our lives, our brains have gathered information from our experiences and created mental maps of connections. If we experience something negative, the brain created a connection from that event to the negative thought or feeling. It is common for our brains to recount that negative experience if we encounter a situation that has similarities to the first. This subconscious process can be overridden by active redirection. Assessing your current situation and highlighting the differences will help your brain to see that this current situation is unique from the past and stands alone. From there the information you receive as you move through your new situation will help to create a new mental map. You can actively choose to transfer knowledge gained from past experiences onto the new experience, sifting out any aspects that are inapplicable.

With a plan for addressing the obstacles and an intentional choice to have positive beliefs you are empowered to make your dream a reality.

> *With a plan for addressing the obstacles and an intentional choice to have positive beliefs you are empowered to make your dream a reality.*

2. MOVING THE DREAM INTO ACTIONABLE STEPS

Once you believe in your dream and are ready to handle the challenges, it is time to plan your strategies and specific actions.

Evaluate and obtain a clear picture of where you currently stand. Be honest and accurate with your assessment. This is the starting point for your plan. Accurate placement leads to increased accuracy and efficiency in your process. Next list options, opportunities, passions, goals, values, and dreams.

Add to your list over several days. When your list is complete, sort your thoughts into categories. Summarize each category in a single sentence.

Once the brainstorming phase is over, the next step is to research. There are many roads that can be taken. Some plans of action may require more research. Utilizing the question, "How can I achieve this goal?" will help to identify alternate courses of action. For each time the question "How?" is asked, there is the potential to identify a new course of action. Proceed until there are at least three options. Evaluate which process will work best for you at this time and then organize your plan.

Keep in mind that some goals run concurrently. To become more efficient, streamline. For example: You have a financial goal of saving money and a health goal of eating healthier. One process for combining both goals is to create a weekly meal plan that allows you to use your time wisely by making multiple meals that are nutritious and stretches your food budget.

The next step in moving your dream is to clarify what you will work on by creating a scope for your actions. Be specific on the things that you will focus on and those that will be outside of your focus. For example, imagine you are seeking to obtain a professional license. To obtain the license, you are required to pass an exam. To prepare for the exam you complete several study modules which are estimated to take six months.

Normally, in your spare time, there are days when you meet up with a friend at the gym and others when you attend a sporting event or committee meeting. In order to accomplish the goal of obtaining the license, you determine that it is best to dedicate at least eight hours a week to study for the exam. In creating your scope, you will identify the days and hours you will dedicate to studying. If an opportunity were to arise that conflicts with this schedule, you seek to reschedule or suspend participating in the activity for a period of time. Once you have accomplished your goal you can return to your normal routine.

The concept of defining your scope can also be applied to smaller actions such as determining which work activities and emails to attend to today, and which activities and emails to defer to tomorrow or subsequent days.

After you have identified your scope, determine what is required to accomplish your goal. Once the requirements are identified, organize the requirements by separating them into categories of beginning, middle, and end. The requirements that must be met first go into the beginning category. This category will also include any prerequisites to initiate your goal. The middle category will include actions or items that you require that build upon the preceding category and guide you toward the end category. The end category consists of final actions or items required to complete your goal. Once categorized, return to the beginning category and prioritize your steps.

Finally, locate resources, gauge their availability, and engage those that are accessible. Take action by focusing on one step at a time. Make changes where appropriate as you gain feedback through the process.

BE PREPARED

Accounting for both expected and unexpected life events is important to the goal mapping process. Challenges, setbacks, and changes in circumstances will happen. Brainstorming and identifying some of these in advance will help you to formulate contingency plans. Consider the question, "What will I do?" if a particular part of your plan works out differently than anticipated. Timeframes or resources may be altered. In some cases, the picture may change entirely and a new goal may be appropriate. Mental flexibility will give you the ability to withstand the changes, adapt quickly, and manage your emotions.

> *Mental flexibility will give you the ability to withstand the changes, adapt quickly, and manage your emotions.*

RISK TAKING AND THE POWER OF MARGINS

An important aspect in achieving your dream is to reach beyond your level of comfort and familiarity. New tasks require learning and risk taking. With this understanding comes the empowerment to step out into the unknown and press on to the vision ahead. During the learning process it is important to be patient, humble, and to persevere.

Recognize that mistakes and discomfort are part of the process and consider them learning opportunities. The objective during this phase is to learn from the mistakes and make peace with the discomfort. There are seasons for everything and eventually, change must and will happen. Discomfort can be an early indicator to initiate plans to prepare for action. You can position yourself to be ahead of change. When the season shifts you will be ready to move along with the current of change rather than against it.

Take risks wisely, research, and create action steps for how you will implement your plan. Some mistakes in your process can be avoided by seeking the expertise and wisdom of others who have passed through similar goals. Include in your support group people who are positive, courageous, disciplined, and assertive. These qualities will prove very helpful as you move forward through the plan.

POTENTIAL GAINS

"What can I gain from this action?" is a question to ask before taking action. Contemplating and brainstorming all of the potential positive outcomes will boost momentum and give you reasons to support your aspirations. It is human nature to seek preservation; taking a risk may appear to threaten our sense of security. In the long run, taking calculated risk leads to more opportunities, resources, and increased stability. The sacrifice in the beginning can lead to major gains along the way, especially if sacrifices are made wisely.

CONFIDENCE

Confidence is crucial to success. Everyday your internal dialogue will indicate how you see the events of the day, how you will respond to the events of the day, and how you will feel about the day. Confidence empowers you to take chances and do something different. Confidence supports the thought pattern that goals are achievable and it inspires you to push until you get satisfaction.

> *Confidence empowers you to take chances and do something different.*

Choose to be positive and confident. Believe in yourself and in the times when you want a boost of encouragement, revisit your journal and reread the notes you made about your past successes. Find time and opportunities to be around people who are also being proactive and striving to make their dreams a reality. Their confidence will help feed your confidence.

CONSISTENCY

Repeating a behavior consistently over time leads to habit formation. A major component of building momentum is building consistency in actions. Many goals have steps that must be repeated and maintained in order to see long lasting results. Whether it is consistent budgeting or performing pushups regularly, change and improvement takes time. There are many methods to build consistency. A popular method is the use of a calendar or tally chart to measure each time you repeat the desired activity. Reminders are beneficial while the habit is being formed. Stick reminder notes where you will see them often. For those who prefer technology, electronic tasks and reminders are quite convenient. They can be easily synced with other daily tasks via web tools.

Another method is to remain in the present, also known as tunnel vision. Your attention remains on the task at hand, disregarding anything else that that is less than an urgent priority. This method helps build focus by purposely choosing to leave tomorrow in the future, yesterday in the past, and dedicating all of your attention to the task at hand. This method is akin to creating a scope; it is applied at an elemental level with the focus being on the moment rather than a longer period of time. It is the act of redirecting current thoughts in a certain direction. Practice remaining in the present for fifteen minute intervals at a time. Increase your intervals as you become more comfortable.

A third method is the use of verbal affirmations. Verbal affirmations can effectuate motivation and positivity. Speak consistency into existence. Speak aloud, "I am doing it" and follow through. If you are seeking to modify your diet, speak it aloud and begin researching meal plans. Then prepare a realistic shopping list for your upcoming week. Shop and stick to the plan.

> *Verbal affirmations can effectuate motivation and positivity.*

Embrace the concept of mini-projects. It will take upwards of three weeks to develop a habit. Create mini projects that span at least one month. At the end of the month, assess your performance by measuring your progress and comparing your results against your target. Consider your project goal and any improvements that may lead to your desired results. What activities will you continue with in the new month? What activities will you change? Identify the changes that will be implemented in the new month. Once your appraisal is complete, take action to move forward into the month.

One important tip to keep in mind with consistency is that it is different than the pursuit of perfection. It is possible that there will be days missed and errors. For each time, get back on track. Periodically you may want rest from the schedule; recharge and reassess your action plan. Decide in advance what you will do to get back on track.

The action plan you create with awareness of risk, confidence, and consistency prepares you to move forward effectively.

3. LEVERAGING RESOURCES

Identifying resources supports belief in a dream being achievable. Planning how to use your skills and tools plus engage other people is foundational to your ultimate success.

> *Planning how to use your skills and tools plus engage other people is foundational to your ultimate success.*

One of the most powerful resources to develop is a support group. Think of family, friends, mentors, or colleagues who have accomplished at least one thing you also want. Connect with them and ask questions. They may have advice or suggestions that will help you in your journey. Network and build connections with people who can support and encourage you through your process.

Another important resource is money. Money will be a requirement in your pursuits. Identify how much it will take and ways to secure it. Creating a separate financial plan and budget is strongly recommended. This chapter is designed to help you process through and create a basic plan for any type of goal, including a financial plan.

Be open minded and flexible as opportunities for support may come in many forms. Commonly resources become available through service to others. Volunteering and giving back to society in any fashion is an excellent way of positioning yourself to receive support.

THERE IS ONLY ONE YOU

You are your most valuable resource. You possess the capacity to be an influence on society in your own unique way. Embrace who you are, leverage your strengths and supplement your weaknesses. Work with your temperament and personality rather than against it. There is increased satisfaction and a smoother process when your actions are aligned with who you are and what you value. When listening to the feedback of others, ascertain what you are capable of doing and how well you fare in those conditions.

> *You are your most valuable resource.*
>
> *When you recognize your own strengths and follow through with your positive beliefs you do have the opportunity and ability to achieve your dream.*

When you recognize your own strengths and follow through with your positive beliefs you do have the opportunity and ability to achieve your dream.

CONCLUSION

To map your dream, start with a vision, faith, wisdom, resourcefulness, and a basic plan. Ensure that the plan is elastic and moldable for it to work. As you move through life events and circumstances you will want to adjust, discard, redirect, or re-envision the plan. Prepare to think on your feet and be willing to take chances.

When you are executing a plan, make a decision to start. Pick the first step and execute it. By organizing the dream into little pieces, you are making the dream manageable. Have confidence that each piece will eventually fit. There are outside events and occurrences that may arise; being flexible empowers you to adjust steps and the big picture. Make the big picture living and dynamic.

Dreams at conception are exciting. With commitment, proper structuring, and action, dreams can become reality. We are all created with a purpose and dreams often point to that purpose. Dreams abstractly display ways in which we can express ourselves and leave an impression on the world. Usually we have more than one dream that we can pursue and many of our dreams can change as time and circumstances in our lives change. The key is to be proactive and remain in pursuit of your dreams. As you move toward your dream, assist another person in achieving their dream.

As a coach, a crucial part of my dream is to help you pursue your dream. I have met with countless people who admitted to having dreams they want to pursue and then claimed that they did not know how to bring them to fruition. This chapter was written to be a beginner's guide to creating plans that will bring many of those dreams into reality.

Shaddae Renee is a Certified Professional Coach with The Center for Coaching Certification.

She is a graduate of Wisconsin Lutheran College with a Bachelor of Arts Degree in Psychology and is currently working toward the completion of a Master of Science Degree in Leadership. She has eight years of experience working in the financial industry. In her spare time, she enjoys spending time with her family and pursuing her passion to help others pursue their dreams.

In 2011, she started her company Apprehend with the mission to help clients of all ages grasp their dreams by assisting them with the creation and execution of goal maps for their personal lives, career and finances. She offers a wide range of services from individual coaching, written literature, to seminars and public speaking.

CoachShaddaeRenee@gmail.com

Career Coaching for Students
Amanda Quayle

A day before I completed my coaching certification I was sitting at a hairdressing salon in Vancouver having my hair cut. Instead of absently flipping through the pages of gossip magazines to see Beyoncé's latest hairstyle or Tay Tay's latest squeeze, I had been musing over the past six weeks of coaching classes. One re-occurring thought kept circling in my mind. I drafted a text message to a close circle of friends, whose opinions I valued highly, and with nervous excitement I hit send. The message was simple, "What guidance can you offer to a graduate looking for their first job?"

As the responses flooded back in I felt privileged to gain their valuable insights; each reply was unique and varied based on decades of work and life experience. There was one common thread repeated in each response. "I wish someone had told me this when I was starting out." If my close group of friends were all echoing the same words, then surely hundreds, if not thousands of graduates, are currently flying blind and simply hoping to get it right as they venture forward without a blueprint for their oncoming careers.

What if I can help them navigate the complexities and challenges in taking their first steps out of high school or college and then arm them with the confidence, knowledge, and insight I've gained throughout my personal and professional career?

For students, graduation marks the beginning of many choices. Sometimes scary, bewildering, thrilling choices. Their life, which once seemed so secure, is now unstable with impending change. Do you remember when you graduated? How did you feel? What happened next? How did you get there?

A major life step like graduating can induce anxiety, create trepidation, or instill fear and confusion. Alternatively, it can conjure up feelings of curiosity, excitement, and adventure as they step out into the unknown. All of these emotions are common when you are completing one stage of your life and embarking on an undetermined next phase.

It is during this time of instability that students will look for support on this journey and consider engaging a career coach. This is likely to be the student's first step into their independent adult life, and the first time they have worked with a career coach. I liken the process of a student participating in career coaching sessions as similar to going on a mountain hike.

Imagine waking one morning after a restful night of sleep. Filled with energy you open the window and feel the warm sun on your skin, see the sky is a bright blue, and sense the air is crisp as you breathe it in. You look out across to the mountains in front of you and decide the weather is idyllic for a hike. Bursting with excitement about the adventure ahead, you grab your backpack, fill it with essential items to survive the elements, pack the car, and you are ready to drive out on your adventure.

As your car approaches the mountain, feelings of doubt creep into your mind and your excitement is replaced with fear. This is your first time hiking in the mountains! You begin to focus on the fact you have zero experience in the mountains and question the validity of your decision. How do you prepare for a hike? Have you packed the right equipment to sustain your day trip? What path will you take and what point do you want to reach? What obstacles can you expect and how will you overcome them? How will you get there? What will you gain from this experience?

> *How do you prepare for ...?*

These questions are much like what a graduating student is asking themselves. To explore possible answers to these questions we will examine six steps in the process of coaching students.

EXPLORE

Where are you now? You reach the mountain and park your car, grab your backpack, and turn your head towards the sky. A canopy of trees forms an umbrella above you, birds are chirping, and you take a deep breath to steady your nerves. A large trail map stands stoic in the car park so you walk over and see a large red dot that says *You Are Here*.

In the first coaching session with a student I ask, "Tell me about yourself." Listening to their answer is crucial to understanding the client and where he or she sees themselves right now in their life. Each student will have his or her own way of explaining who they are and respond based on the way they think, feel, and act. By focusing on what they say and how they say it, I gain clarity on where they are now.

Looking at the trail map, you can see the full picture of your current location. Markings show the existing hiking trails and their difficulty, picnic tables, streams, lookouts, rest stops, caution areas, and points of interest. With this information you determine what your next steps are and how to navigate where you want to go.

For some students this trail map may be crystal clear, for others this may be a confusing and unsettling time. I find the initial questions for getting to know the client are powerful tools to further understand them individually. To obtain a holistic overview of a student's current mindset you want them to share information about their family, friends, relationships, study, occupation, recreation, and personal motivation.

All of this background knowledge assists you in learning and understanding your client. Students are unique individuals; they think, feel, and respond differently. Their personality, communication style, and perspective are considerations when coaching them. As coaches, we recognize these differences and ask the student questions based on who they are and where they see themselves as individuals. By doing this we help guide them to their next step.

NAVIGATE

It's time to start the hike; how will you determine where you want to go?

For a student considering their future this can be a daunting task, especially when they are unsure of the answers. Confident students will be clear about their destination whereas uncertain students may want more help to navigate this next step and determine where they ultimately want to reach.

I will ask the student, "What goal or goals do you want to achieve?" The answer usually unfolds in two ways. The first is the student has yet to determine any goals and your role as their coach is to work with them on figuring this out. The second is the student is very clear on the end goal and at the same time unsure of the steps to get there. Maybe their goal is to earn $60,000 a year, travel the world blogging, change their major in college, find a specific job, or start an online business.

There are a few tactics I employ to help a student determine their goal or goals. The first is to ensure all questions are open-ended, empowering the student to talk freely about their goals. Leading questions influence the response so open questions are vital to encourage a student to work through the process of determining where they want to go. Open questions foster independent thought and generate authentic responses that ultimately empower the student.

> *... ensure all questions are open-ended ...*

The second tactic is considering the student's personality and their reaction when you ask, "Where do you want to go?" Is their reaction aggressive or passive? Is it emotional or logical? On a hike the aggressive, self-assured student may skip reading the map, make a quick decision, and select any trail to see where it takes them. A passive student is likely more cautious, taking the time to research and analyze every trail before making a decision on where they will hike. An emotional student will trust their gut and instinctively follow where the path goes. The logical student will map out their path, plot rest stops along the way, and estimate time of arrival to their destination.

Whatever the student's approach, it is imperative as their coach that you remain open-minded and support them on their journey. The process is for them to navigate and uncover their own path. This is their hike after all! Based on their response you are able to adapt the way in which you coach them to create their plan and achieve goals.

It is important to note that even on well-marked trails experienced hikers continue navigating. While a student may be clear and focused on where they want to go, there are external circumstances that occur along the journey. You may find yourself coaching confident students to navigate risks and find alternate routes to help them get to their ultimate destination.

The third tactic is helping the student describe their ideal experience or what their world will look like once their goal is achieved. Ask, "How will you feel? What do you see? What do you hear?" This emotional, sensory connection makes thoughts vivid and tangible, supporting students realizing there are options and feeling open to possibility. Visualizing themselves reaching their destination is empowering.

Finally, encourage the student to face forward just as they do on the hiking trail. When you are looking forward you can see the signs ahead showing where the path goes. When you are looking backward or sideways you are unable to see ahead clearly and there is more risk that you trip and fall or injure yourself. The same concept applies with coaching. Coaching focuses forward, on the future, and what can be controlled. Therefore, encourage the student to focus forward and envision where they want to go, and the path will open up before them.

> *When you are looking forward you can see the signs ahead showing where the path goes.*

DESIGN

What do you require to get there? You see a waterfall marked on the map as a point of interest and decide this is where you want to go. It is hilly and challenging terrain, and the reward is you will experience a beautiful sight and feel a great sense of achievement at the end of the day. What do you do?

Designing a plan to get you from the base of the mountain to the waterfall is much like a crucial stage of the coaching process. I use the word designing instead of planning as it is more active. Planning places the emphasis on writing a list and ticking the items off. Designing is fluid and there is room for evolution and change in the process, even when your end goal is clear. Designing brings your personal concept or idea into realization to achieve an objective.

In this stage of the coaching process I ask the student to identify the skills and experience they believe are required to achieve their goal. What's their fitness level or mindset to be successful? What do they want in their backpack to help them successfully achieve their goals? What are the student's expectations about the timeframe?

This varies for every student and examples of what it will take may include:
- creating a resume,
- practice interviewing for jobs,
- speaking with friends and family about career possibilities,
- networking to explore opportunities in the industry they want to work in.

It may also include personal development such as seeking financial advice, talking to a therapist, completing additional training, committing to a regular fitness regime, building a professional wardrobe, or gaining experience. Once gaps have been identified, actions can be clarified.

> *Once gaps have been identified, actions can be clarified.*

The next step is to ask students to detail their current skills or experience. This question encourages personal analysis and inward thinking about their abilities, what they are passionate about, attributes, skills, and past experiences they can draw upon to achieve their goals. Students may have backpacks brimming with a variety of tools they have forgotten to use or leverage.

Some students will be unsure about what equipment they have in their backpack or, in other words, unsure of what skills and strengths they have, let alone what they are passionate about. Maybe they have self-confidence challenges, learning difficulties, or perhaps they dropped out of school early to work and now want to return to studies. Maybe they felt uninspired at school and spent their class time daydreaming. As a coach I find the combination of empathy, understanding, and using open questions to be useful when encouraging a student to discover and share their attributes.

Furthermore, I partner with students so they write their skills down to reinforce a positive mindset. Students can use their skills in a positive way, write mantra's, and re-visit their writing to reinforce messages until they have embodied them.

Great activities to undertake during the designing process include brainstorming, writing checklists, researching, and continuing to ask those open questions! Students are the architects of their future; as coaches we are there to help them design the blueprint for their action plan.

DISCOVER

What will motivate you to get there? You have decided to hike to the beautiful waterfall, you know what path you are taking, what obstacles you face, and what skills and strengths you can call upon. Now, what will keep you motivated on your journey to the waterfall? What do you want to achieve along the way as you move toward that final destination?

When a student is designing a plan to achieve their goals, a valuable step is to ascertain their priorities. As a student there can be many competing priorities: assignments, family, finances, socializing, sports clubs, relationships, religion, specific interest groups, or volunteering. Having a variety of activities in your life is great to manage stress, plus feel well rounded and balanced as an individual. The key is to prioritize those undertakings so that the end goal is supported.

> *... there can be many competing priorities ...*

I ask students, "What could prevent you from achieving your goal?" This question invites them to review what is going on and identify any potential road blocks along the way. It also sets up the opportunity to ask them the follow-up question, "What will you do to move past these obstacles?" This question brings awareness to the student to acknowledge what challenges may occur, then consider how they will take responsibility and manage them.

After they identify the things that could potentially prevent them from achieving their goal, I ask them to focus on the options they have to stay motivated and achieve their objective. Asking the student to use proactive language and describe what tasks they will employ to maintain motivation brings conscious awareness of achieving their goal. It is ultimately their intrinsic motivators that will keep them on the trail.

If a student finds it difficult to think of motivators you may brainstorm ideas together. Music, food, visiting or calling a friend, creating a vision board, and establishing mantras with positive and inspiring words are all practical suggestions.

TRANSFORM

Imagine you are hiking to the waterfall when you pass a sign that reads *Scenic overlook – 1 mile*. You stray from your original path, persuaded that you will see another beautiful sight. Thirty minutes down the track you realize you are lost and dark clouds are hovering. The first few drops of rain wet your arms and you look for cover to find the only shelter is the surrounding trees. You turn back the way you came with blistered ankles rubbing against rain soaked shoes, tired, hungry, and defeated.

As adults we experience obstacles and difficulties throughout our life. For a student who is oblivious to these prospective incidences, how do coaches prepare or support them when unplanned change occurs?

Problems might arise at work or home or they may have a general underwhelming feeling about where they are on their journey. How do we help them re-focus on what they want to achieve?

Transformation plays a vital role in what unfolds after a hurdle is surpassed. At times our clients may feel stuck, sad, or lost. This is completely normal and we as coaches have experienced these feelings in our personal lives. Sometimes people jump to frantically try anything and everything to find purpose. Instead, pause, take a deep breath, and evaluate. What have you learned on your journey? What do you want? Look for options or possibilities for next steps. Like caterpillars along a hiking trail, sometimes it helps to move slowly, taking time to build a cocoon before evolving into a gorgeous butterfly and taking flight.

> *What have you learned on your journey?*

During this transformation period it helps for the coach to ask the student to identify the barriers or obstacles that they faced and discover new insights. What are they learning? What happens when viewing the situation with a different perspective? What do they want to change about their current situation? How will they change it?

I also remind students to be kind to themselves and realize that even the best hikers can get lost, fear failure, or have their confidence shaken. That it can be appropriate to stop and rest, re-evaluate, gather one's thoughts. When they have had time to re-focus on where they want to go they will feel ready to carry on. They can get up, dust themselves off, and move forward to take on new challenges. It is through this process that the student will grow, refining his or her sense of character, and build resilience for tackling the next phase.

EVALUATE

What did you gain from this experience? As you walk back down the mountain, legs aching, cheeks flushed from your day outdoors, you look out and see the sun melting into the horizon. You have had a day filled with adventure and while things may have taken an unplanned turn, you still feel a sense of accomplishment. This morning you were a novice hiker, full of fear about the unknown challenges that were yet to come. Now you have a multitude of new experiences and learnings about who you are and what you can achieve.

Reflecting on the day, you consider the positives and negatives of your experience. What will you do differently to prepare for the next hike? What options and risks will you research? When will you explore alternative routes? What do you want to learn to be a better hiker? How was your goal realized?

Achieving a goal is the capstone for any client. As a coach our role continues after the client reaches this pinnacle. When goals are realized it is the time for us to help the student look back at their experience and evaluate. This is an opportunity for the student to consider what learnings they gained from their experience and how they will carry them forward.

Encouraging a student to verbally share their evaluation of an experience leads them into deeper reflection. By recalling their experience, they actively consider how to improve processes, identify skills they require, plus learn how to manage adversity, stress, and setbacks. Through evaluation they learn to ask for help, trust their instincts, change direction where appropriate, and find solutions.

Ask the student how they have changed throughout the experience. Perhaps they achieved their goal easily or maybe their original goal changed as they were moving along the path, just like it did on the hike to the waterfall. How did they adapt? How did they identify the new way forward? What did they focus on? What setbacks did they experience? How did they overcome them?

If students are struggling to find solutions I will ask them if I can help through a joint brainstorming. Ideas I add can be as simple as preparing a contingency plan, learning new skills, continuing to seek out new experiences, and meeting new people.

When I brainstorm with them I am sure to add several ideas, invite more from them, and put them in charge of decisions or choices. Explore ways to ultimately grow as a person. I like to ask a student, "What did you learn about yourself?" and encourage them to answer using positive language.

Reflect back on your own life and consider how many times change has occurred. Change is certain in life and our experiences, environment, and the people we meet along the way all contribute to influencing us on our journey. Our plans and goals reflect who we are at different stages of our lives. As coaches we support clients to design and redesign priorities depending on the stage of life they are experiencing.

This chapter explored how a coach supports a student; I want to break from that momentarily and flip the mirror on ourselves. Consider your role as a coach: how will you be the best coach for your clients? Ultimately coaching is about helping people realize their potential by defining goals and actively setting about achieving their objectives. So how do you bring your skill set and strengths to deliver on helping your client achieve their unique purpose?

Personally I find that to grow and develop I seek out new information on coaching regularly. Both in coaching and also subjects that spark my curiosity and make me want to read, write, watch webinars, and bounce ideas off friends and fellow coaches.

After a coaching session I evaluate my own role in the session and with a dose of healthy introspective examination look for ways I can improve my communication and listening skills.

> *After a coaching session I evaluate my own role in the session and with a dose of healthy introspective examination look for ways I can improve my communication and listening skills.*

I design and re-design my goals and actively work towards them by using mantras. I choose to show up for myself, deliberately and consciously using positive language.

There are times when I feel unmotivated to do anything other than be in a mellow mood. So, I listen to B.B. King while I silently cook dinner or turn up the stereo loudly and dance wildly in my living room, rocking out to ACDC until my husband comes home and tells me I'm making the neighbors deaf. It's all an effort to be true to myself, and listen to my mind and body better.

As coaches it is important to be healthy and happy so we are in the best position possible to support our clients. If you evaluate your own position and be true to yourself, then your authenticity will radiate and you will be building empathy, rapport, and trust with the people you serve, your clients.

Our journey, similar to our clients, is non-linear. There are peaks and valleys to our progress in our careers as coaches and that's perfectly normal. There are going to be weeks where things feel stagnant, hard, and the dots aren't connecting. That's ok. Because there's also going to be weeks where things seem to be progressing full steam ahead and everything is humming smoothly.

We can be truer to our clients if we are also wearing a backpack filled with skills and resources, equipping us for an adventure. It is then that we will be able to prepare them with the best tools and knowledge for the summit that awaits.

Amanda Quayle is an Australian, living and working in Sydney. With a Bachelor's Degree in Communications, her 14-year career spans Australia, Cambodia, Macau, United Kingdom, and the United States. Amanda is experienced in managing marketing and communications teams in not-for-profit, corporate, and government organizations. Her passion is supporting women in their career development.

In 2015 Amanda became a qualified coach with the Center for Coaching Certification. She partnered with a previous colleague, Carmen Walsh, who shared the same ambitions to support women. Together they launched Quayle & Walsh Career Specialists. Q&W is a female-focused career coaching service dedicated to help women realize their full potential and kick start their careers with confidence.

Q&W offers services for recent graduates from high schools, universities, and MBA programs that are seeking to accelerate their professional futures.

www.quaylewalsh.com

CAREER GAME PLANS
Julie Kratz

HAVING A PLAN INCREASES YOUR CHANCES OF SUCCESS

Research shows that when you have a plan, your chances of achieving career success are 80% higher. Think about the power of this insight: those that set goals for themselves achieve higher rates of success in their careers. Knowing what you want and having a plan to get there is pivotal.

Whether it is taking your career to an even higher level, pivoting industries or functional areas, or advancing to a leadership role, high potential women in career transition wrestle with having a solid game plan to facilitate their success.

When coaching women in career transition, I believe that there is a solution to this challenge: The Career Game Plan. It is a simple four-step process. It is unique to each person and defines what success looks like. It fits on one-page and is easily shared with managers, mentors, and coaches. It paints the picture of what good looks like, with a clear road map to get there. First, it means being able to articulate what you want, and what you are uniquely skilled to do, your purpose statement. This in turn helps you define goals to support your purpose coming to fruition. Next, you will brainstorm the competencies that feed your success. Finally, you will define the action steps to achieve your goals.

Picture a tree: its roots, trunk, branches, and leaves. In many ways the Career Game Plan process resembles a tree. Purpose statements are the roots. Your purpose is the basis for everything you do. Your purpose is deeply connected to who you are and what you stand for, strengthening over time. The roots feed the growth and a strong tree grows outward through its branches, which are similar to the goals of your plan. A tree's branches have a strong base to rest on and through which they are fed, the trunk. The trunk is vital to the stability of the tree, just as your competencies are for your plans. Competencies are the skills, behaviors, and/or attributes that support how you will fulfill your purpose and achieve your goals. Then, a tree expands beyond its branches with its leaves. These are the shorter term action steps you take to achieve your longer term goals. With a strong base of roots, the tree grows. Just as a strong purpose helps grow your Career Game Plan. Here's a visual to illustrate the process.

Let's unpack the four essential elements of a winning career game plan: 1) a purpose statement, 2) goals, 3) competencies, and 4) actions. We will start with your purpose statement.

CRAFT A PURPOSE STATEMENT

To build your own winning career game plan, start with knowing what you want. This is summarized best in a purpose statement. For this to be done well, the statement must be concise. Think of Twitter tweet length, which is 140 characters or less. People's attention spans are increasingly short, and if you get too long winded, you risk losing people's interest and interfere with their ability to comprehend your purpose fully. A good quick test is running it by those you trust and know well, and asking them to paraphrase it. If they understand what you stand for and what you want to do, and are able to play it back for you accurately, then you know you are on the right track. A strong purpose articulates your passions, your unique strengths, and your essence in a single sentence.

Your purpose statements often become the beginnings of your networking elevator speech. You want to know them by heart, and proudly share them with a confident smile when asked the infamous question, "What do you do?" Perhaps when you are asked this question you, like many others, noticeably experience an internal struggle. It appears as if something fails to jive, and as a result, fails to roll off the tongue naturally. Perhaps you feel that internal struggle between sharing what you do versus what you really want to do. People can read your body language and see that you are being less than completely genuine. It comes across as a lack of confidence and it is really holding your back from what truly excites you professionally. In order to connect in a meaningful way and make others happy, start with being happy yourself.

> *In order to connect in a meaningful way and make others happy, start with being happy yourself.*

When you feel this internal conflict, it is a sign you are not following your true purpose. To overcome this, take a look in the mirror and do some soul searching. Purpose statements have three key elements: your passions, your strengths, and your unique capabilities. Reflect on what makes you truly happy and excited, asking these questions:

- What types of tasks, meetings, or work are you doing on your favorite days? What do you enjoy working on? The answer to these questions will likely yield some of the sources of your true happiness and your passions.
- How do you describe your talents in your resume or on LinkedIn? How do other people describe your talents? This signals your strengths.
- What subjects do people ask for your help or advice on? This is a strong indicator of your unique capabilities.

There is no secret recipe to discovering your purpose. While passions, strengths, and capabilities often are the nuts and bolts of these statements, each statement is unique and meaningful to the person. Think of them as concentric circles rather than a linear algebraic equation. Some words might overlap with other words; some elements might live independently.

To do this, using the questions above, generate a bank of twenty or so words. As in a true brainstorm, all words are good words. Let them all flow, with the personal challenge to brainstorm as many as possible. Then, once you have a complete list of possibilities, begin looking for similarities and differences. One option is to use post-it notes for this exercise, organizing separate words into different themes or groups based on similarities, creating separate post-it groups based on differences. The goal here is to create groups of words that are mutually exclusive from one another and collectively exhaust all possible words. These groups become your themes. Take the groups and weave them together. It's like knitting a quilt of different patches. They are unique words that when brought together create more value. Take a step back, and think about the big picture: Who are you? What do you want? What makes you happy? The themes bridged together become your purpose statement. If the purpose statement answers these questions succinctly, you've got a winner.

There are many successful applications of purpose statements.

Many use them in networking settings, social media descriptions, website profiles, resume headers, bio beginnings, and more. Some of my favorites are:

- I get to make dreams come true through facilitating the process for people to find their dream homes.
- I am passionate about fostering growth by offering authentic resources and inspiration on how to navigate the entrepreneurial waters so that women can set their own standards for success.
- I collaborate with diverse teams to build winning strategies that increase employee engagement and business performance.

At my business, Pivot Point, this has evolved over time. It currently reads, "Pivot Point exists to develop leaders and coach high potential women in career transition through building winning Career Game Plans." By testing it with others, and through feedback, it has continuously improved.

Here are some tips to cementing a good first draft before moving onto the second step of goals. First, feedback is a gift, especially with your purpose statements. Share them with those that know you best, and pressure test them to be even better. If you say it with a smile, and it feels genuine, you are in great shape to move onto step two. Secondly, recognizing that these statements often describe your future self, there are likely areas to be developed. The statements are intended to be aspirational. What we mean by this is that the purpose statement may encompass your opportunities for future success. Often, people find that there is a gap between what they want and what they are doing. This leads us to your next step, which is all about setting appropriate goals aligned with your purpose statements. This is what takes your career to the next level.

> *Often, people find that there is a gap between what they want and what they are doing.*

BUILD GOALS

Now that you have the first draft of your purpose statement, it's time to build the goals to actively fulfill it. Keeping with the analogy that your Career Game Plan process is like a tree, your purpose statements are the roots.

To take your purpose from aspirational to real, strong goals are pivotal. We recommend setting two or three goals, and definitely no more than three that you are focused on and working actively toward at any one time. We have consistently found with coaching clients that when you set more than three goals to pursue at once, it becomes very difficult to focus, thus lowering chances of success. Just as you did with your purpose statements, brainstorming up front is key. Let the goals flow out of you, involve those you trust in the brainstorm, and let your purposes guide you during this process. With every potential goal ask yourself, "how does this help me fulfill my purpose statement?"

Your goals are the guard rails on your Career Game Plans. They help provide boundaries for what you do versus what you do not do. Jumping forward to the fourth step of your Career Game Plan, the goals also help you prioritize your tasks. When you are deciding what to prioritize on your task list, or whether to meet with someone or attend a networking event, remind yourself of your goals, and ask how this action step helps you achieve it. If it does not have a high likelihood of helping you achieve your goals, then do not prioritize it. Goals lend focus.

To set good goals, we like the SMART goal framework: creating goals that are specific, measurable, actionable, relevant, and time bound. Once you have prioritized a handful of goals, look at these like a checklist to make your goals even better:
- Specific: What specifically will happen to achieve this goal?
- Measurable: How will you measure the successful achievement of this goal?
- Actionable: During the time frame specified, how will you take action to achieve this goal?
- Relevant: How relevant is this goal to your purpose?
- Time bound: When will this goal be achieved?

This is a very popular framework and with its popularity comes some drawbacks. Some versions of SMART goals use the word attainable for the A. While goals must be specific and measurable so that you clearly know when you achieve success, attainability is a controversial one. You want to be realistic with your goals, and balance them with optimism. You do want to ensure the goal is relevant for you and your purpose because that in turn feeds your ability to create the outcomes. Then, having a time-bound component (months, years, etc.), draws the line in the sand for when you will measure it. A best practice is to have clear timelines for all of your goals, that way it is crystal clear how often to measure and sets you up to celebrate success, an important motivator to keep going.

As an area of awareness and consideration: we find that our clients often limit their own success with negative self-talk. For example: "There's no way I could do that," or "I will try to do this." The words you tell yourself matter. If you use limiting language in your goals, then you limit your ability to achieve them. We like this example of a goal, "I will grow my new business to a $1 billion in ten years." When we use the SMART checklist, it's specific and measurable with $1 billion, it is actionable by defining the specific steps to take, it is relevant assuming the person is a primary business owner, and it is timely in ten years. This is where sub goals come into play. Break out larger, more daunting long-term goals into shorter term, attainable goals. What that looks like in this example is, "I will grow my new business to $1 million in year one, $5 million in year three, and $1 billion in year ten." Obviously, financial rigor is appropriate to fine tune the numbers. Perhaps you decide that while the $1 billion is achievable, it is the time frame that may shift to make it realistic.

Another option is to fine tune the numbers. You can decide to change the numbers based on your planning horizon over the next one to three years. You are far more likely to achieve success when you set challenging and also reasonable goals up front. Tell your brain that success is within reach, even if you are unable to see the finish line. Then, focus on your purpose statements, skills and competencies, and your action steps.

Goals often include financial measures as appropriate such as revenue, profitability, number of clients, number of products or services, and client satisfaction ratings. If financials are not what you want to measure, we recommend thinking about what you can measure, and what indications you will watch to determine how successful you are in moving toward your goals. For example, a client I coached wanted to grow her own retirement services business. Instead of using financial metrics, she chose to focus on number of clients and referrals. You have choices. Stretch your thinking during this exercise. Remember, you have your action steps as the final step where you will identify the tactics. If you find yourself getting too tactical too quick, we recommend identifying a basket of activities or tasks like marketing presence, professional development, or relationship building, and then building a higher level goal from there. Items like website development, social media strategy, and partner organizations are very tactical and likely will be action steps within the larger long-term goal.

Once you have a strong set of goals that align with the SMART goal framework, you are ready to prioritize how you will achieve them. This will include using your skills and resources for taking specific action steps.

PRIORITIZE COMPETENCIES

Remembering your tree analogy, the competencies represent the trunk. The trunk is the stable center that connects your purposeful roots to your far-reaching branches, or goals. They provide an extra layer of focus for connecting your vision of your future success with the goals to actively fulfill it. Competencies are the skills, behaviors, or attributes that define who you will become. They range from leadership skills to detail-oriented attributes to communication behaviors. They ensure your ability to achieve your plans, and help strike a balance between your high level goals and purpose statements.

When you reflect on your purpose statements, it is likely that there are elements of the statements that you will be achieving later, in the future. Your competencies help you close those gaps. Even if you are actively living your purpose statements today, utilize your skills to further strengthen your already strong roots or purpose statements. It is one thing to have goals to get there, it is another to have a list of skills and/or behaviors to internalize to make it possible. These are often unique to a profession, industry, or functional area. In coaching, we find that having business acumen, confidence, influence, active listening, empathy, and powerful questioning competencies are vital for success.

> *... utilize your skills to further strengthen your already strong roots or purpose statements.*

Just like with your goals, having too many competencies limits focus and your ability to truly make a considerable impact on that competency. Again, we recommend prioritizing three competencies to focus on developing and using that have both a high impact on your purpose and goals, and also that you have a high ability to improve upon.

The example I use often is being detail-oriented, which is a known weakness of mine. This is important at times when I take notes, do social media, and write thought leadership materials. This known weakness does have relevance to my goals and purpose. In my situation, rather than focus on a known limitation I choose to outsource these activities. I choose to focus on other competencies, like influence and confidence, that move the needle on impact and I have a higher probability of improving upon.

The Nielson Group published an article, "List of Soft Skill Competencies with Description," with a menu of more than 100 possible competencies to choose from. We encourage perusing it with your purpose statements and goals in mind. Select all of the competencies on the list that will have impact on your success. Then, with list in hand, prioritize the list based on your ability to improve upon the goals and the purpose and the impact of the competency. A number of techniques work well here: simply voting, rating each factor on impact and ability, weighing against decision criteria, or making a 2x2 matrix with decision factors. I like keeping it simple, and as long as the top three competencies have a considerable impact and are within reach, you likely have a good combination to take your career to the next level. Competencies help you align your training activities and often dictate your professional development budget allocations. You will prioritize activities in the final step that ensure you are building upon these skills, attributes, and behaviors to fulfill your purpose and achieve your goals.

DETERMINE ACTIONS

You have arrived. You are on the final step of building your winning Career Game Plan. A nice reward for taking the time to invest in a purpose statement, SMART goals, and prioritized competencies, is that this step is fairly effortless. If you have diligently articulated your purpose, crafted goals that fulfill it, and chosen to focus on the competencies that drive the most positive impact on those, your tactical plan emerges naturally. Just like the leaves emerge each spring on a tree with a set of strong roots, a stable trunk, and healthy branches, so too do the actions for your plans. With a strategic plan, you will easily set in motion the steps to achieve your goals.

> *If you have diligently articulated your purpose, crafted goals that fulfill it, and chosen to focus on the competencies that drive the most positive impact on those, your tactical plan emerges naturally.*

Action plans have three key ingredients. Again, in the spirit of keeping things simple, there is some magic to keeping to the rule of three. In this case, solid action plans have: 1) the action step name and description, 2) the resources to achieve it, and 3) a timeline for completion. Take each goal and break it down into smaller steps, then create a column for resources, and another column with a deadline completion date. If an action step requires a significant time or money investment, it is essential that the investment be a part of the plan early on, especially since other stakeholders, like your managers, significant others, and partners may be involved in helping you achieve your plan. Completion dates are key for accountability. When you write a date down beside a goal, you increase your chances of success by 80%. Putting pen to paper makes it real. If timelines move out, that is okay; document the step.

It is important to accept that the elements of your action plans are subject to change as you learn more. Start big, and fine-tune based on feedback. Time and money are finite resources, so be mindful about what you commit to, while also thinking big.

For example, imagine you have three years to achieve your plans. The beauty of this process is that you can break down your goals into your desired time frame. For example, break yours down by three month blocks of time, and keep a running to-do list on your office white board or in a journal. Everything that makes the three-month task list supports your long-term purpose and three-year goals. It is the filter by which you prioritize your action steps. From social media, to speaking events, to conferences you attend, all must highly impact your goals and be aligned with your purpose.

Action steps are checklist items that you clearly define with exactly what you are doing, how you are doing it, the resources you will use to do it, and by when you will have it done.

Bringing it all together, you now have a proven process to build your winning Career Game Plan. When you dedicate the time to the process, your plans take root and you branch out, growing with each successful meeting, project, or initiative. I challenge you to celebrate those success milestones because that feeds your growth. When you cross a big to-do off the list, or complete an action plan, ask yourselves this powerful question, "how will you celebrate success?" Make it part of your plan to think of rewards and recognition mechanisms that motivate you to achieve success again. Your brain will naturally find ways to achieve success again; it's self-fulfilling. With every choice you make, you take a step closer to having the career you truly want. Remember, those with a plan win.

Now, how will you build your own winning Career Game Plan?

Julie Kratz is a Certified Master Coach and Kelley MBA with experience in operations, marketing, and strategy in the manufacturing, financial services, and agriculture industries. Throughout her twelve years in corporate America, Julie has been recognized for excellence in facilitation, strategic thinking, and leadership.

Julie is the author of the book, Pivot Point: How to Build a Winning Career Game Plan. As a new mother, having experienced her own pivot point mid-career, Julie started her own coaching business, Pivot Point. Pivot Point exists to develop leaders and coach high potential women in transition through building winning career game plans.

By nature, Julie is collaborative and driven by measurable impact with her clients. She is passionate about helping leaders and women with their "what's next" moments in their career and leadership journeys.

Download your Career Game Plan Workbook, join the Community Newsletter, and sign up for your first complimentary coaching session.

www.NextPivotPoint.com

When It Is Time for Feedback
Linda Clark

From the moment you are born, giving and receiving feedback begins. There is every reason to expect you will be accomplished at both giving and receiving feedback. At the same time, over and over again, many of us discover that receiving feedback is a learned skill.

Some of this may be due to the environment you are in. If you are exposed to poorly-delivered feedback, if there is disinterest in the value of receiving feedback, or if you are taught that the power lies with those giving the feedback, you may miss out on a skill that creates growth. Once you enter the workforce, carrying your perspectives and experience, you enter a realm where the ability to accept and act on feedback becomes an indicator of success and in many cases an expected competency.

The choice to pursue coaching may come as a result of feedback. Certain conversations may lead to directed coaching to enhance performance, or self-awareness may lead the client to the coach as part of their next steps. My experience working with students in communication and leadership clients, both organizational and personal, and additionally my work as an HR professional continues to reinforce that feedback is both a frequent subject in business environments and often one of the touchiest. Most of us take great pride in how we give feedback by aiming for responsible, considerate discussions framed in constructive ways.

> *The choice to pursue coaching may come as a result of feedback.*

This chapter explores the influence of feedback reception on our ability to advance our careers, be coached, effect change, and be in a place of self-awareness for future improvement. I will review some of the consequences and unintended outcomes due to the inability, or unwillingness, to be competent in feedback reception. If a weakness exists in the feedback reception skill, it is usually undiscovered until the feedback is received. Following that review is a four-step process to unpack the interference from feedback and move forward proactively.

THE DRAMA OF IMMEDIACY

Immediacy is generated when a response is demanded as part of the feedback discussion. This can be challenging as the receiver works to process the input, create a personal organization for the feedback, and then realizes there is an expectation for response. Despite the admonishment that it's just not personal, feedback is deeply personal.

The drama of immediacy is the dissonance that can occur between the speaker's abilities to construct and deliver quality feedback in a range of circumstances versus the listener's developed response to receiving feedback. The fluid ability to deliver feedback in a range of situations crafted in cohesive and constructive formats is completely separate from an equivalent reception skill.

When you discuss communication competencies in business environments, it is often the skill of receiving information that is the most challenging. Certain skills form the foundation of multiple competencies for leadership. The more visible skills are often the ability to provide feedback, manage difficult conversations, and being results-focused. Common topics include emotional intelligence, relationship competency, and transformational leadership styles. The training is strongly focused on giving the feedback and being in the authority role.

When it comes to receiving information, the star of the conversation is often active listening. Active listening also supports a number of competencies in the interpersonal range. Active listening is a learned skill. Receiving feedback is more than active listening. Consider that the receiving of feedback is also an active process, that can be practiced and developed into a learned skill. In active listening, we filter out unnecessary noise and bring ourselves, mindful and present, into the current discussion. Actively receiving feedback can become a learned skill of taking us from a place of hearing feedback and disruptive noise around the feedback, and into the role of consumption of the feedback, then actively engaging in the process of acting on the feedback. A consideration for noise is that we often generate internal noise and interference that is fully as distracting as any external noise. The active process helps to overcome distractions and noise.

CONSEQUENCES AND UNINTENDED OUTCOMES

The consequences and unintended outcomes of feedback reception impact self-awareness and the ability to use feedback to improve. Within organizations, the ability to accept and integrate feedback becomes a hallmark of your reputation. A resistance to feedback may actually increase the importance of receiving it.

> *Within organizations, the ability to accept and integrate feedback becomes a hallmark of your reputation.*

As business cultures evolve, the relevance of interpersonal skills has grown. Cultures now exist where the expectation is continuous feedback and improvement. The changing structure of organizations assigns more value to relationship capital. This is evidenced by the pursuit of organizational communication programs in universities, the rise of coaching as an investment in talent development, and the focus on interpersonal skills over technical expectations. The technical capacity to perform the duties of the job is merely a minimum.

The rise of the organizational champion is based on a fluid combination of technical ability, interpersonal skills, feedback cycles, and relationships.

> *The rise of the organizational champion is based on a fluid combination of technical ability, interpersonal skills, feedback cycles, and relationships.*

Resistance to feedback occurs at multiple levels ranging from momentary fear of being shamed through active forms of resistance, including belligerent outbursts or workplace bullying behaviors. Resistance to feedback may stop the flow of information and create voids where information is missing. Regardless, the importance of feedback remains. If you resist feedback you may become, in the perception of others, uncoachable. While it is unlikely that someone is truly and permanently uncoachable, the perception of the leader, the colleague, or the customer can create the label. In the realm of success in relationships, being held as resistant, reactive, or uncoachable is a barrier to success.

Consider resistance and two possible types that may manifest in the feedback discussion: active and passive. Active resistance may display as argumentative, dismissive of the feedback, or a counter-attack from defensiveness. This pattern of response, and professional notoriety, is often a foundation for employees to be selected for remedial training or even counseling.

Passive resistance manifests as avoidance or dismissal of the feedback, often based in opinions about the quality of the feedback, the messenger, or the importance of the message. With passive resistance, the recipient may declare that they listened to the feedback and that is the extent of their action. With very personal feedback, listening without reaction most likely means missing opportunities.

If a coaching relationship is created with a resistant client and feedback is addressed, resistance may continue to influence the dialogue. If the client has been directed to participate in coaching to address a required improvement, there may be resistance to the notion of coaching. Understanding that the feedback has value and committing to the process of going forward to actionable behaviors may be delayed due to resistance. Although the investment in coaching is often a vote of confidence on the part of the organization, directive situations may begin as tense, resistant situations. At the start of this kind of coaching relationship, the skill of the coach to establish trust and rapport is essential. The coaching process supports the positive transition to determining outcomes and generating appropriate actions to result in improvement.

As an example, think about any personal areas of development or improvements you have recently made, or have in mind for the future. How receptive were you to changes suggested by others versus changes you made in an independent matter as a function of your self-learning or self-improvement? This self-reflection often helps to identify our own forms of resistance, the triggers that may drive such resistance, and how to build skills that increase receptivity.

Action: Take a moment to consider the following statements, and your reaction to them:
  A. I want to lose some weight and be more fit.
  B. It will be good for you if you lose some weight.
  OR
  A. I want to work on my interpersonal skills and confidence.
  B. People think you are difficult; what do you think about that?

The difference above is the difference between defining what you want as happens in coaching and being told as happens with poorly given feedback.

Current trends in organizational development and workforce planning show that organizations are moving away from the annual performance evaluation and into active feedback cycles that occur in real-time to create course correction moments early and be flexible. More and more, the concept of waiting to provide feedback, reward, or correction is seen as interfering with business continuity and agility.

> *... organizations are moving away from the annual performance evaluation and into active feedback cycles ...*

As future leaders are discussed and selected, the candidates are often the best at feedback acceptance. This is generally a function of an environment accepts and celebrates the other looming f word, failure. Such an environment realizes failure inevitably occurs when new, creative solutions are explored.

This compares to accountability moments in the coaching relationship where results are discussed, challenges identified, and any changes or next steps are established by the client. In the one-on-one coaching relationship, this environment of exploration and safety with multiple solutions is a great parallel.

> *... results are discussed, challenges identified, and any changes or next steps are established by the client.*

BEWARE THE MESSENGER

At this point, we've talked about the reactivity of the recipient of the feedback. Now consider the value of the feedback delivery being skilled. The delivery of the feedback can be compromised from the skill of the individual providing the feedback, intent, or environmental conditions such as noise or others in proximity. Part of the reaction to the feedback is often an assessment of the validity of the message and the competency of the messenger.

We have developed ways to communicate that receiving feedback is going to be a difficult experience. Although feedback can easily be positive, we tend to reserve words such as compliment or praise to mean positive feedback, and retain feedback as the word to mean that unpleasant news is coming. The conversation, especially in the hands of someone with minimal feedback delivery skills, may begin with, "Don't kill the messenger!" or "Listen to what they say, not how they are saying it!" Neither phrase creates a sense of a safe and collaborative environment for improvement; instead this creates a sense of tension for those delivering feedback and that they are carrying a negative message. Avoidance and resistance can appear on the delivery side of the feedback cycle as well.

Action: Think about the last time you received feedback from someone who was emotional or unskilled in the process, and recall your immediate response. Which of the following options, if any, might have changed your feedback response?
a) The same feedback came from a different person.
b) The feedback was delivered differently by the same person.

The choice may be a clue as to resistance about feedback. Teenagers have been proving for years that the best feedback comes from someone other than the parent, linking relationships and credibility. With the second option, tone and timing play major roles in whether we receive feedback as constructive, caring, appropriate, or with our best interests in mind.

The Positive Transition

Whether working with a coach or alone, there is value in creating action steps. If you know that accepting feedback is a stressor for you, taking the time to work on this in an environment that is calm may be just the ticket for your success when feedback comes. Clients are often able to tackle the most difficult of topics with grace and aplomb when they have that personal power of choice to prioritize the topic. A change in perspective may be the best first step to receiving feedback differently.

We engage in cycles of giving and receiving opinions on a frequent basis. This casual interaction is often a goal when organizations create coaching and feedback cultures. Being exposed to something more frequently often increases our skill level and reduces any sensitivities to the perceived difficulty.

Introducing a framework that structures the feedback reception experience from receiving through application supports receiving feedback as a skill. Using a four step method that I refer to as CORE, feedback can be analyzed with appropriate decision-making applied. The goal of CORE is to unpack the noise and interference, discard emotional layers or stories, and arrive at the message contained within the feedback.

CORE removes the drama of immediacy by building in process

steps. It creates space for exploration and validates that many things may be going on in the feedback process. CORE is marked by four phases that distill information in a funnel format, with each phase progressively smaller and more focused.

The four phases are:
1. Consume: The reception portion of the dialogue.
2. Organize: Beginning immediately after the input.
3. Respond: An outward step of feedback reception.
4. Execute: Decision and action implementation.

> *Consume. Organize. Respond. Execute.*

Using CORE creates a mindful approach to feedback reception, being fully in the moment when receiving information while knowing that a structured process will follow for arriving at an actionable message. CORE's greatest strength is guiding the transitory process from the moment of feedback to the readiness for action.

PHASE 1: CONSUME

Consuming content is meant to describe an awareness of content and how you choose to interact. At any moment you may be processing content in several ways. Consuming content is more reflective of the totality of the interaction with the content.

Shifting this perspective to feedback, the first step is to consume all of the available feedback. Our willingness and ability to consume feedback determines how much feedback, and likely the investment in the quality of feedback, we receive. A common reaction during feedback reception is that an editing process begins while the feedback is in process. Unfortunately, this process reduces the message, possibly filtering important data. Consuming the feedback in its entirety is important.

Much like the onset of the coaching process with the discovery mode looking for the broadest responses and areas of focus, this consume stage is about grabbing the content, message, supporting dialogue, and all details. At this time, remaining open to receiving the details of the message is a best practice.

It is important when receiving feedback to work towards gaining an understanding of the message. Critical questions at this point involve understanding the goal and outcomes of the feedback. It can be tempting to linger in the source or the emotional fodder of the feedback; that interferes with a positive transition.

Take notes; the consume phase will easily be the largest section of your process. With each successive phase, you will organize and refine the information into pieces that contribute to your future goals. The concept of consuming the feedback brings you into the closest contact with the entire message and will empower you to analyze the message at a later time. The survey of perceptions comes at a later point, and postponing analysis allows mindfulness during the data portion of feedback.

> *... postponing analysis allows mindfulness ...*

PHASE 2: ORGANIZE

When the feedback concludes and you have the opportunity to begin processing, the organize phase begins. During this time, it is very important to separate an analytical decision to dismiss components of the feedback from an emotional response.

Positive transition begins by holding the feedback in your hands, holding it up to the light, seeing how the light turns and reflects, and seeing it for what it really means. Discover the message, the value, and the goal of the feedback.

Consider organizing as the first step in a puzzle. You are making sure you have all the pieces, in a work area, turned face up, and you think about a strategy for putting the pieces together.

The signals near the end of organizing and preparing to move to response include having an idea about how you want to respond to a primary insight. How does your self-reflection prepare you for wanting to take action on the feedback? It may be that feedback requires no additional action. Your response and execution phases may be reduced to a simple decision to dismiss the feedback. The decision of acting or dismissing is based in your personal set of priorities and values.

PHASE 3: RESPONSE

There are several Response decisions that may be warranted after your period of organizing is over. Consider the importance of a response to the person who provided feedback. The execution phase may include follow up discussions, an email reflecting your understanding, or a phone call. What response to others that might have been involved in a situation, a decision, or a pattern of behaviors is appropriate? That response may also be planned.

The response phase is best after the mulling over of the feedback and indeed any personal wound-licking has ended, the actual message has been identified, and personal accountability for involvement has started.

PHASE 4: EXECUTE

In the response phase external communication and response start. In the execution phase new strategies and actions are implemented. In execution you may see additional involvement of third parties such as development coaches, career strategists, therapists, or counselors as appropriate for improvement areas identified in the first three phases. Execution may include ongoing feedback and continuing to refine the goals and process. In each phase, more extraneous steps and information are peeled away and the execution phase becomes concise and focused.

THE FINAL EXAM EXPERIMENT

I've had the pleasure of teaching undergraduate Group and Team Dynamics and we spend a great deal of time in the semester discussing feedback, challenging the status quo, and open communication. The class focuses on communication, dividing into small groups for the semester. This encourages the life cycle of groups and teams, including tensions and conflict management.

The students are part of Organizational Communication and Strategic Communication majors and will go on to work in human resources, business leadership, public relations, advertising, and more. They have spent the better part of three or four years focused on interpersonal, organizational, and strategic communication in their communication major areas. Typical to the parallel in the business environment where giving feedback is expected, the class was quite comfortable with providing feedback and opinions. In complete solidarity with many of us, they became nervous or reticent about receiving feedback.

Throughout the semester as we worked on group and team dynamics, they had opportunities to provide feedback about projects, exams, group dynamics, and more. As a group, we decided to informally test exposure and familiarity with feedback as a way to ease into the CORE process.

Rather than sit through a tedious and traditional final exam, we formatted a practical exam based entirely on feedback. The exam was structured in three sections.

Section 1: The teams sat together in pairs for 15 minutes in open feedback discussions, giving and receiving feedback about observed team dynamics, roles within the teams, quality of presentations, and areas of improvement. At the end of each 15 minutes, the teams rotated until all groups had met.

Section 2: This section shifted to individual feedback and continued in the face-to-face model with pairs set up in a speed-dating format. Students sat together for 2 minutes of rapid feedback about their individual observations and performance over the semester. A timer counted down the 2 minutes and then a rotation occurred. This continued for 45 minutes.

Section 3: Students then quietly wrote individual reflections on the feedback and submitted those to me.

What was the point and purpose? The students stayed in the consume phase of CORE for nearly two hours. They fully received feedback in multiple formats directly and publicly. Their reflection papers reported that nearly 80% of them had personal shyness or insecurity about receiving feedback dissipate within 10 minutes of beginning. They felt this caused them to gain confidence and comfort based on several factors:

1. The proximity of others also going through the cycle and having immediate validation that others were nervous participating and struggling. Discomfort was normal. In that state of normalcy, it became comfortable.
2. The generation of empathy for the challenge of the situation and also the personal investment to providing constructive feedback to respected peers.
3. The time constraint created a task environment for them and allowed the release of emotional attachments around the process of giving and receiving.
4. The immediacy of time, performance consideration, and speed created an environment of presence and mindfulness. The self-talk censors shut down and students experienced emotional acceptance of being validated.

In that state of normalcy, [discomfort] became comfortable.

The longer term outcome is students in their first jobs after graduation report a higher comfort level with receiving feedback in their new environments and confidence with having a model for processing feedback in their relationships.

COACHING THE FEEDBACK TRANSITION

The CORE feedback process may be outside the coaching process. The outcome of CORE may be a desire to discuss the feedback with a coach, develop an action plan with a coach, or have an accountability partner.

While clients are free to explore emotions and root causes in their own CORE process, or with appropriate resources, the coaching relationship is about future state. Clients may use coaching to prepare for and address the phases of CORE. Since feedback is designed for future improvement, coaching and actionable feedback are aligned.

One of the most valuable moments in the coaching relationship occurs with interruption. While we are taught early that interrupting is rude or inconsiderate, the measured interruption in coaching is a powerful moment of accountability.

> *... measured interruption in coaching is a powerful moment of accountability.*

The interruption in coaching is used when the emotion of the feedback situation may reappear, or when looking back is the focus of the story. The timing of this interruption brings the focus back to the present, creating a pause and space for the client to recognize where they are and how they want to move forward.

Previously we considered the requirement of coaching in an organization; it is equally or more important to consider elective coaching. In elective coaching, where feedback might be brought up, it may or may not be a priority or area of focus for the client. Feedback touching on personal triggers may be as sensitive as other challenging areas.

In a directive process, especially with a requirement for corrected or improved behavior, there is a call to remain focused on the area. If the client is stuck, it may be helpful to explore with them how close they are to being able to move out of resistance or avoidance and into actionable behaviors for improvement.

A question I've used for exploring where the client is after receiving feedback is the simple approach of, "What do you want to do with this information?" This opens a wide range of responses that may include doing nothing, setting an action item to revisit, or wading into the topic as a current priority. The coach is flexible to any direction the client chooses.

When any type of forward motion results from this question, it is a great sign about where they are in the feedback process. If still in the throes of emotion, responses may have disempowered or avoidant language, such as, "Nothing, it was stupid anyway," or "I don't know what they expect from me!"

For the coach, possible next steps may include asking follow-up questions such as:
- What do you want to work on?
- How does your reaction impact your work and career?

THE ELEPHANT IN THE ROOM

One of the clichés we hear when tackling a large project or problem is that you eat the elephant one bite at a time. We talk about the elephant in the room when discussing issues of avoidance. My own initial response has been, "Why are you inviting elephants over?" and "it's not very nice to eat them anyway!" The fear and resistance you can feel with feedback may feel like a double whammy of avoidance of the elephant in the room and determining how to address and resolve the elephant. All of this can be wrapped with emotions that lead us to withdrawing or finding another way to cope.

Several factors are at play in the receiving of feedback. Covered here is the initial reticence, nervousness, or full resistance to receiving feedback, and the resulting consequences of the inability or unwillingness to receive feedback. Critical to the success of each person are the developed skills of receiving feedback, appropriate editing to arrive at the correct purpose and goal of the feedback, removing extraneous detail provided by either party, and arriving at the best decision for how to act upon the feedback.

Before a plan is established it is important to consider the client perspective on tackling feedback with or without a coach, and the coaching perspective of tackling feedback with a client. Willingness and consent from the client must exist. The decision about feedback belongs to the client.

Given the growth of focus on interpersonal skills, the self-learning for any person means a significant portion of time spent on evaluating a balanced range of feedback skills from both the giving and receiving side, an ongoing method of practice and development, and a willingness to revise based on feedback. Feedback is personal. It's a personal opportunity for decisions and considered actions best for personal growth. Take it as personally, deeply, and actionably as suits your goals.

> *Feedback is personal. It's a personal opportunity for decisions and considered actions best for personal growth.*

Linda Clark owns an organizational development and transformative coaching firm focused on transition and change through authenticity, peak performance, and personal presence. In addition to individual services, she provides group and organizational services focused around change management, growth of culture, and leadership development when aligned with business objectives.

With nearly twenty years of business management experience, most concentrated on strategic human resources practices and organizational development in Fortune 500 automotive retail and energy sectors, she built a reputation of being operationally focused while building respect and empathy at all levels. A passionate focus on service to other drives an engaging presentation style focused on learning-centered environments, filled with storytelling and humor for best audience engagement.

Mrs. Clark holds a B.S.in Healthcare Business Administration from the University of Central Florida and a Master's degree in Human Resources Management from the University of Phoenix. She is a Certified Master Coach through the Center for Coaching Certification and has been coaching for more than 3 years. She has held her SPHR certification since 2005 and has facilitated exam prep courses for 10 years.

www.executivechameleon.com

COACHING THE ATHLETE VERSUS COACHING THE EXECUTIVE
Emily Bass

Coaching dates back to tutoring and sports since the 1800's. In its simplest form, these types of coaches are defined as "a person who gives advice." The beginning of many definitions of a coach is "a person who teaches or trains..." This is changing with the popularity of professional coaches such as life, health, business, career, and executive coaches. When looking at what an executive coach does, it is similar to the sports coach in many respects and also differs in precise and important ways. What follows is a comparison and contrast of the sports coach, in skiing specifically, to the executive coach, as I experience it.

A sports coach focuses on the athlete and their performance, providing guidance, training, and support. Similar to a sports coach, executive coaches support the client; in contrast executive coaches ask questions so the executive creates action steps and goals based on what they wish to achieve.

What differs is the executive coach doesn't tell or advise; instead of direct involvement from the coach to set the goals, the client is the sole decision-maker. The executive coach recognizes the client has the answer so asks open-ended questions prompting the client to discover the answer themselves. The executive coach listens to understand and to know what to ask next in order to provoke more thought on a particular subject identified by the executive.

Another difference is that the sports coach is a teacher with a student. Teachers provide advice and direction, telling the student what to do and how to do it. Executive coaches partner with clients so the client explores, moves past obstacles, strategizes, plans their own actions, and creates the change as defined and chosen by the client. This highlights an important difference in the relationship between an executive coach and the sports coach: an executive coach is a partner there to empower the client.

THE COACHING RELATIONSHIP

One's relationship with their coach, whether for sports, health and fitness, work, or career, is of the utmost importance. The value and effectiveness of the coaching relationship are based on openness and honesty where vulnerability is accepted and even expected. Sometimes the student of a sports coach looks up to them as a mentor and role model, even a philosopher of sorts. Most athletes will tell you they tend to perform better when their coach is present supporting, analyzing, and providing feedback. With executives their coaches play more of partnership role, typically only present before and after an event such as a meeting. The power of the relationship often follows the executive into the meeting, providing a sense of supporting presence.

> *The power of the relationship often follows the executive ...*

When asking coaches about how they view these relationships, the sports coach often responds that they think of their students as protégés' or mentees. Sports coaches express their respect for their students, and the courage and dedication students have to their sport and their body.

The sports coach, being a coach because they have often reached the level of expertise in the sport themselves, respects the process the athlete is going through. They understand the motivation, determination, and focus required to train and attain the level of skill to be a professional athlete. The sports coach relates to the whole-body/whole-person commitment to their sport and their body as their tool, and that is part of where the value of having a coach comes in for the athlete.

The relationship between the executive and the executive coach has similarities in many respects. Executive coaches express that the respect they have for their clients comes from the very reason they are there to coach—the executive's commitment to successfully navigate the business world's challenging terrain and increase their company's bottom line. An executive's dedication to their mission, responsibilities, the people involved, and the community at large is impressive and to be respected. Often it is the day-to-day existence that is the most impressive to the executive coach. Just as the day's performance on the course for the ski racer is the ultimate impressive element of the athlete's performance, the day's performance in a meeting or challenging encounter can be the ultimate impressive element of the executive's performance.

The coaching relationship, whether for the athlete or the executive, requires trust and honesty for the student/client, with their success as the ultimate goal.

> *The coaching relationship ... requires trust and honesty ...*

An important role of the sports coach is the ability to literally see and analyze the performance of the athlete. In a sense, the athlete is performing blind and their poor movement patterns are blind spots. Unless athletes see themselves on video, they are literally unable to see themselves. Similar to the athlete, it can be challenging for an executive to see themselves and how they appear in the field. What differs is that the type of blind spot is based simply on their humanness instead of physical performance; each produces its own type of vulnerabilities.

My take on the executive's blind spots boils down to learned coping patterns, ego, unwise intentions, confidence, or politics. Athletes also deal with having to overcome learned patterns (of movement), ego, confidence, and competition—in fact, these things are huge barriers to success. It is different in the sense that a physical vulnerability such as athletic performance is concrete and tangible with clear goals for change, whereas leadership vulnerabilities may be more personal, more about who the person is and how they are in their world, which creates a vulnerability much harder to see and admit to as well as change. Another difference that stands out to me is that for the athlete, it is most often when they reach the top level of their field that they deal with these issues whereas the executive often deals with such challenges throughout their development. Having a coach to help manage these challenges is important for both the executive and the athlete, with the strength of the relationship being essential to effectiveness.

Both the athlete and the executive face fear. Many blind spots are based on fear. The skier leans back when they are hesitant or afraid of the terrain or the speed they are gaining. I think that is an accurate statement and a good analogy for the executive as well—they lean out from, instead of in to, the table or the conversation or the situation when the terrain is unfamiliar, picks up too much momentum, or gets bumpy.

This is where the coach adds value by implementing the delicate skill of creating awareness. For example, creating awareness of when in the process their fear started to set in. The awareness may be as deep-seated as the use of learned survival behaviors in their family unit or in their social circles, or it may be as superficial as being inexperienced with a particular situation; similar to the skier's fear when approaching unfamiliar terrain.

One executive I worked with shared she took on the role of mean girl in school and learned not to trust people because of witnessing gossip among her friends. This learned behavior is very similar to what an athlete experiences if they learn poor movement patterns such as muscling one's way through the bumpy terrain instead of balanced alignment for flow through the bumps. The way past these learned patterns of behavior are also similar for both the athlete and the executive through supportive coaching to create awareness of challenging patterns and changing to positive ones.

The ski coach provides the resources in the form of physical skill building for the skier, knowing what terrain to put them on to practice those skills in order to own them and build confidence. The executive coach helps the client explore situations and resources, and mirrors back what the executive is sharing, empowering them to see themselves. Both types of coaches provide guidance so the student/client can reach the top of the mountain without breaking their own leg or anyone else's, if that is their goal. The difference in the relationship with the coach for the executive is that the executive has the answers whereas the athlete does looks to his or her coach.

> *The executive coach helps the client explore situations and resources, and mirrors back what the executive is sharing, empowering them to see themselves.*

The relationship between coach and student/client is based on trust and respect. The student/client must feel comfortable being vulnerable and confident the coach sees them completely.

SETTING AND ATTAINING GOALS

Setting goals and how one attains them differ between the athlete and the executive. The skier may tell their coach their overall goal of wanting to ski all the intermediate terrain comfortably. The ski coach then identifies the gap in skills and creates stepping stones for their student, telling and showing them what and how to do it. They encourage and provide feedback throughout, even skiing with them to literally mirror proper movements for them or manipulating them physically to feel the correct moves.

The executive coach questions, providing space for the client to explore possibilities and express how they see, feel, or think about things. An executive coach focuses on the client's impressions and asks about other possible perspectives. It is a conversation to provoke thought and empower the executive to define their goals and direction. Executive coaching includes mirroring also; it is mirroring the client's words back to them and asking for more.

The executive coach focuses on repeating the positive statements or rephrases in an affirmative way so as to support clear, positive, proactive thought patterns; similar to how the sports coach performs the maneuvers in the correct way, leading the student to see positive movement patterns with the goal of creating the correct image for the student. Through open-ended questioning, the executive coach listens to what the client says so they can identify what the client wants. They then take the very words of the client and reflect them back.

The scope of goals for an executive is broad and can range from any issue in the person's life to one particular project in a particular area. This broad scope arena for goal options means the look of success for an executive is just as broad. The coach for the executive then uses their fine-tuned skills in helping the executive to clarify and pinpoint and prioritize goals. Through further questioning to bring out existing resources and strengths, the executive coach helps the client identify action steps and timelines as well as measures for success.

Awareness is enlightening to the executive, just as it is to the athlete. The sports coach analyzes movement and then teaches and advises. The executive coach brings about awareness through discussion, plus exploration of their client's wants, thoughts, and behaviors. Both the client and the athlete are empowered to set goals with attached action steps and timelines for making change.

RISK TAKING AND CHANGE

In sports, risk and change involve learning a new skill in the physical sense for the most part. When taking risk, for the skier it can mean physically stretching limits. For the executive, the risk can be reputational, financial, or even loss of work. For the athlete, the consequence is failure for self or team in the particular race and perhaps losing one's spot on the team. For the executive, the consequence may also be losing a spot on the team or project.

Goal setting for the athlete is sometimes perceived as concrete in comparison to the executive; the same thought applies to change when looking at physical change versus behavior change. I am referring to physical change as movements of the body in performance in a sport and behavior change as actions of the mind and as a result, behaviors.

The athlete is primarily making changes physically. There is psychological and emotional determination as well as sportsmanship and confidence-based change too. For change to occur in sports, the athlete has the opportunity to practice it with their coach; they are guided in the moment of performance to remember it, visualize it, repeat it, see it, feel it, and take it to new terrain and new heights. They practice, repeat to learn deeply, and expand by testing at a higher level of challenge for a longer period of time. They explore, fall, and get back up.

The consequences may be harder and the risk greater for executives. When a ski racer wipes out and breaks a leg, we think they are brave and they gave it their all. When an executive crashes because they took a chance, the perception is often very different—they don't have what it takes or they can't be trusted with a new project. Building skills for the athlete and the executive comes with very different risks.

SKILL BUILDING COACHING A NOVICE VERSUS AN EXPERT

The skills are tangible and physical for the athlete and the path to getting there can be somewhat linear. Certainly, there are emotions to overcome and commitment to practice in the behavioral sense; the tangible outcome and the linear path make the path to success different for the athlete than for the executive. Skill building for the executive can be somewhat more emotional or behavioral in the intellectual sense. Muscle memory is a very different behavior change than is management style, writing, communication, and public speaking skills.

The athlete builds skills that allow them to physically perform within a very specific framework whereas the executive builds varied soft skills that are applied in many different situations.

Coaching a beginner skier is not that different than coaching the expert. Using skiing as an example: the expert skier still encounters fear of being hurt and even of looking silly, just like the beginner skier. At the same time, the beginner thinks more about survival whereas the expert thinks about efficiency and finesse. When working on learning new skills it can be intimidating because falling is often the best way to learn, creating vulnerability for the expert.

> *When working on learning new skills it can be intimidating because falling is often the best way to learn, creating vulnerability for the expert.*

The different expectations for the new and the seasoned executive are similar to those of the skier's. The novice executive is still developing and polishing skills and the expectation may be that they will experience fear and end up flailing. Similar to the novice skier, finding challenging and new terrain is easier for the new executive and they still think hard about how they execute their newly found skills. Just like the expert skier, expectations for the seasoned executive are that they smoothly navigate any terrain. When it comes to the stages of learning, there is much similarity between the skier and the executive because those stages apply in all types of learning.

I often use the metaphor of driving the stick shift when talking about levels of learning and skill development:
- Stage 1: Unconsciously unskilled: One does not know what they don't know about driving a stick shift until they try to do

it. There is no real measure whether they have the skills.
- Stage 2: Consciously unskilled: They get in the car and most likely pop the clutch and are unable to drive the car. They now know what they don't know. They experience failure and can now measure their abilities. This creates frustration and perhaps a loss of confidence.
- Stage 3: Consciously skilled: The stage where they can drive a stick shift with focused intention even while fear and hesitation abound, especially when starting from a position of stopped and heading uphill. This stage elicits motivation from successful attempts as well as frustration from failures.
- Stage 4: Unconsciously skilled: They can get in the car and drive free of thinking about what they are doing. They have mastered the skill and it happens as second nature. They can talk and drive and drink their coffee regardless of the terrain.

Good coaches focus on success rather than struggles. Coaches focus on small successes and build from them, taking them to the next level of skill development. The beginning states of learning feel like baby steps and even falling backwards; once one gets past the stage of consciously unskilled and experiences successes, they thrive and reach great heights.

Executives commonly request coaching for developing and enhancing soft skills: communication, problem solving, decision-making, teamwork, and adaptability. Skill building is ultimately about awareness. My most successful ski runs have been when I am completely in the moment and present with every single move and feel of my body from one edge of the ski to the other. I prepared and trained for the moment. My most successful presentations and leadership moments in the business world have been when I am completely in the moment with the other person or people in front of me and I am aware of their every word, movement, and expression guiding me into my next move. Just like the athlete, as an executive I prepared by practicing the presentation, having resources, and reviewing notes. Awareness and presence for any type of coach is a key factor for success and it leads to stronger communication because of being in the moment.

> *Skill building is ultimately about awareness.*

COMMUNICATION WITH AN ATHLETE VERSUS AN EXECUTIVE

The stages of learning for the athlete or the executive are the same. Similarly, how the coach communicates with the athlete or the executive is the same in that it is clear communication.

Using the phrase "How does it feel?" when coaching an athlete results in a very different outcome than when asking the same question of an executive. As referenced earlier, for the athlete it is a concrete, tangible feeling when learning a new skill. With an executive it is a more fleeting feeling, an intuition. If the executive is a person who uses the word "feeling" to describe their actions in the business world then they are that type of learner, kinesthetic. If the person is more auditory then the question is more appropriately phrased as "What does it sound like?" or for visual "What do you envision?"

Communication is probably the single most important skill I have worked on with clients. Whatever the type of coaching, establishing communication that invites key words or phrases that hold a pre-established meaning can be of great value. For example, when working with a skier, it is necessary to create a type of code that can be easily repeated while the skier is moving down the mountain. One word, such as fold, can be used to communicate to the skier at the middle or bottom of a turn that they are to begin flexing smoothly so they can absorb the pressure building in that part of the turn. The word and its meaning was established in the lesson part of the process and works as an efficient way of communicating a larger meaning while moving down the hill and in the moment of action.

The same is true for the executive; creating key words or mantras that they can use on their own in a meeting or conflict situation. When moving into the executive world it took time for me to learn how to best match my communication style with those I worked with and that there are clear differences from how I had naturally communicated in the sports world. Similar to sports coaching, analogies can work well to get a point across and provide clarity of meaning in the executive world.

Alternatively, the executive world requires communication that is collaboratively framed and open for discussion and flexibility.

Communication also differs in that an executive coach uses process skills instead of subject matter expertise to develop the skills of an executive. The coach in this scenario is questioning, listening, and reflecting what the executive already knows. They are empowering the executive to unleash their knowledge in a way that moves them toward their self-identified goals.

The difference between the two coaches is in their roles. The ski coach is teaching whereas the executive coach is partnering. The ski coach is telling whereas the executive coach is listening. The skills of the ski coach are about skiing and developing those skills in the student whereas the skills of the executive coach are about fostering already present skills and creating an environment for self-awareness. As a result of this difference, the communication is different.

The executive seeking a coach is most likely in a state of transition, turmoil on the job, learning to be a better manager, or hoping to initiate change within themselves or their company. These things are human things so the humanness of the coach and their coach training for process expertise are what provides the greatest impact. The executive coach has spent as much time as the ski coach mastering how to be skilled at supporting their client in reaching their goals. The communication is different in that the sports coach is communicating what they identify in their student whereas the executive coach is helping the executive to identify it for themselves.

LEARNING STYLES, PERSONALITY STYLES, AND ENVIRONMENT

Whether with the executive or the athlete, take personality and learning styles into consideration when communicating, and be

> *The executive coach has spent as much time as the ski coach mastering how to be skilled at supporting their client in reaching their goals.*

aware of how they change in a learning environment. Most often, I identify with a doer more than a thinker and prefer a faster communication style as well as prefer to communicate quickly to others. My personality style most often aligns with a personality type best described as the celebrator, which means I want to move and make things happen. Recently though, being in the student role in my coach training, I was identified as being more thoughtful and having a personality style of a more detailed person, responding more slowly to answers as I found myself thinking more thoroughly to formulate my answer. This was a surprise to me and it was accurate. Although surprising, it presented an opportunity to experience first-hand the importance of matching one's communication style to one's client's learning and personality style as well as taking into consideration how the coaching environment may alter one's style, just as the learning environment altered mine.

Successful coaching involves the coach's awareness of their client's learning style. It is important for the coach to meet their client where they are in all types of scenarios. A coach meets their client in the moment of any given situation; the coach meets them in their personality style, in their learning style, and in their environment. As the situation and the environment change, so do aspects of one's personality and learning style.

Personalities are made up of many different factors ranging from genetic to environmental. Sports coaches are trained to consider physical ability as well as personality. Take for example a skier who is cautious versus a skier who is an adventure seeker: the lesson plan for a cautious skier looks very different than the lesson plan for an adventure-seeking skier.

Similarly, the executive coach may question in smaller steps, leaving more space for the cautious personality to think about their answers and feel comfortable with exploring and dreaming. In time they develop the confidence and skills to explore more challenging terrain such as deeper self-awareness.

The sports coach creates an environment of success for the skier by ensuring their readiness for the challenge. The executive coach creates an atmosphere that empowers the adventure seeker the opportunity to dream big and the space to think through their goals and action steps so they are set up to be successful.

It is key for coaches to understand the different learning styles if they want to help clients reach their goals. Coaching the skier means demonstrating for the visual learner, explaining for the auditory learner, or having them experience by doing it for the kinesthetic learner. Executive coaches tailor their coaching by asking their questions using words appropriate to the client's learning style: how they see, hear, or feel.

IN SUMMARY

As coaches, we have the skills to support change in our clients. The sports coach does this through exercises and training schedules, creating situations that provide practice and repetition so skills become second nature. The executive coach does this by using the words of the client and asking them for goals and action steps with measures and timelines identified by the client. The executive coach uses positivity and forward thinking statements incorporating the client's words. Then, by checking in and providing accountability, the executive coach empowers the client to develop new skills and create the change they are seeking.

The roots of coaching have grown and expanded. The field of sports coaching has become a lucrative business and has even expanded into recreational therapeutic professions. The field of executive coaching is flourishing into one that I am proud to be a part of because it is respecting its roots while finding its own ground. Being attentive to the importance of such things as relationships, goal setting, and communication in coaching is important to me as any type of a coach. As an athlete and ski instructor first, I find my skills cross over into executive coaching quite naturally. As a clinical and macro social worker, practiced in clinical skills and collaboratives, I find those skills combine with the sports coach and cross over into executive coaching nicely. As I grow my skills through training and certifications in executive coaching I find one way that executive coaching improves is for the coach to be present when the executive is performing; I also realize this requires travel plus planning for the coach to be in the work environment.

Coaching, whether for the athlete or the executive, is a gift for the coach as much as it is for the client. Being sought to coach a high performing person in their quest to improve his or her self is a privilege. I now realize that I followed my calling in each of my careers: sports, social worker, nonprofit, and philanthropy; each of these steps led me to and contribute to the executive coach I am today. It is a gift to have this personal understanding as I partner with others on their path.

> *Coaching, whether for the athlete or the executive, is a gift for the coach as much as it is for the client.*

Success through coaching is about prompting clarity and awareness, whether that be a mountain top or the top of the executive chain. Success in skiing means you do the maneuver and it feels natural, effortless, exhilarating, fun and fulfilling; where you feel you just have to go back to the top for that one more run. Success in the executive world is like that too—excitement for that next project, that next meeting, and that next success while being your authentic self.

Emily Bass is the owner of Emily Bass Strategies, offering Executive Coaching and Organizational Development services to clients worldwide. Emily is passionate about working with clients to personally, professionally, and financially build their legacy, find balance, and reenergize their connection to their mission.

She holds a Bachelor's and Master's in Social Work from the University of Alaska, is a level III certified alpine and adaptive ski coach and examiner through with Professional Ski Instructors of America (PSIA) and Disabled Sports USA, and is a Certified Master Coach through the Center for Coaching certification as well as a member of the International Coach Federation.

Emily has been leading, supporting and volunteering in the nonprofit sector for more than 25 years. Early in her career, she rose to a level III certified alpine and adaptive ski coach with Professional Ski Instructors of America (PSIA). She went on to become the founding director of an adaptive ski school and an examiner through PSIA and Disabled Sports USA.

Combining professional ski coaching, clinical and macro social work, philanthropy program leadership, and nonprofit leadership makes executive coaching quite natural for Emily.

www.EmilyBassstrategies.com

How Coaching Helped a Legacy Business
Kelly Gangl

My recent experience over a period of eighteen months helping a small business undergo a transformational change has revealed to me a richer awareness of reality. I used to believe that successful organizations had leaders with brilliant ideas who smoothly implemented them to resolve the issues in their organizations. I can remember sitting in many break-out sessions at HR and leadership conferences thinking that the speakers made it sound so easy. Was I just choosing the wrong organizations to associate myself with? I used to believe that the organizations I worked for had unusually tough situations or that I just was not coming up with the right solutions. The experience helped me to be more realistic and it has also boosted my confidence and persistence. Let's face it, the situation usually appears worse when you are immersed in the thick of a challenge than when a scenario is presented at a conference. Instead of a magic bullet or even a linear plan that moves an organization smoothly to the finish line, it takes a lot of continual focus on meeting the members of the organization right where they are and also hard work.

This chapter is about my on-going journey with the leaders of a small, century-old business. For the first time in their history, a non-family CEO had been hired to lead the organization and he reached out to me to explore the possibility of working together.

I had recently resigned from a full-time corporate HR position to finish up a Master's Degree in Organizational Development. Frankly, I was looking for a case study for a diagnostic project in school, and this seemed like a good fit. Getting paid was a nice bonus.

This journey provided some of the most difficult and also rewarding outcomes of my career. I believe that this experience and the collective efforts helped to provide a renewed sense of optimism for the organization as a whole. The leaders and the employees were re-energized from having the opportunity to participate in the planning of the company's future.

> *The leaders and the employees were re-energized from having the opportunity to participate in the planning of the company's future.*

It is interesting that neither the CEO nor I had any idea when we first started working together that we were going to end up where we did. It was like starting a trip without knowing our destination; just letting signs pop up as we traveled and allowing the adventures we encountered along the way to be the guide.

Before I share my experience it is important to set the stage for the company's work environment when I started on this project. The company is a contract firm. Many of the employees have been with the company for most of their careers, meaning 20, 30, and even 40 years, and the systems supporting their efforts have also been in place for nearly that long. Several of the business units were physically located in separate buildings so interactions between employees located at separate buildings occurred only occasionally or when there were problems. The leaders of the business units worked separately, reporting infrequently to the CEO, and communication between divisions was rare. I can remember walking into the corporate office and experiencing a quiet environment with mostly somber faces.

I found through this experience that evidence of progress is rarely immediately quantifiable or found as a number on a financial statement. Instead it is revealed through small examples that can be measured by sight, sound, and visceral experiences. This journey provided the opportunity to reflect and learn throughout. I captured a top ten list of insights to share here.

1. **Clients Often are Unsure of Their True Interests**

When first discussing the potential of us working together, the CEO suggested that I update their employee handbook. I asked him what problem he was hoping to solve by updating the handbook and he described his perception that most of the leaders in the company lacked a consistent set of guidelines. He felt that they all worked independently in silos rather than as a unified team.

I offered to meet with all the leaders to collect their feedback and this was the start of a project that made strides towards transforming the entire company. If I had meekly accepted the initial project offered, the company would have acquired a pretty darned good employee handbook, and one which would have had no significant effect on their operation.

2. THERE IS MORE THAN ONE BEST SOLUTION OR PLAN

I had to learn to accept being comfortable with the fact that gathering all the answers is a journey. It was important to manage both the clients' expectations and my own. Many times the leaders wanted to go to action quickly, implementing changes before really taking the time to clearly define the problems and determine the root causes. Because I was fairly new to serving in the role of external consultant and coach, I worried in the beginning that I was failing to add enough value, and possibly even getting in the way. By being patient and using the data we collected to guide us, we built trust within the group and learned to operate in a more methodical manner.

3. THE CLIENT OWNS THE ACTIONS OR INITIATIVES

Early on in this journey, I realized that I had too often stayed as consultant and sold the CEO on my recommendations in private discussion, only to find that I ended up owning the concepts and approaches in group settings. I had to step back and realize that if I stopped trying so hard to promote my ideas and spent more time coaching the CEO and the leadership team to actively participate in choosing the approach, then I was going to be much more effective. As it turned out, that is what he and the team wanted anyway. I learned to back off, ask questions to encourage reflection, carefully listen, and reflect back the critical points. We started breaking through barriers; the CEO helped me to understand when he wanted training, consulting, or coaching. When I followed his timing, it helped me to better meet both his interests and, ultimately, the company's.

> *I had to step back and realize that if I stopped trying so hard to promote my ideas and spent more time coaching the CEO and the leadership team to actively participate in choosing the approach, then I was going to be much more effective.*

I had to change my old habits. My normal approach throughout my career as an HR practitioner was to help others with their problems by coming up with what I thought was the best solution. That often seemed to be a successful approach. I have come to realize that it prevented the people I thought I was helping from growing and taking ownership. When I approached the CEO and other leaders in the company as a coach rather than a solution provider, I was able to listen more carefully to what they were experiencing. I challenged their thinking when appropriate. My focus was on helping them think through the challenges and develop solutions using their own creative thinking. I simply provided the forum that empowered them to slow down and consider what they wanted their ideal environment to look like.

4. IT GETS MESSY SO MANAGE EXPECTATIONS

The leaders and employees involved in any major change initiative will learn fairly quickly that the process involves discomfort and sometimes pain. Some of the participants will buy in early, and feel frustrated that the changes or benefits are emerging too slowly. Others will resist new concepts insisting the way they had been working is fine. Managing expectations from the beginning helps.

By encouraging input, collecting feedback, sharing the results, and facilitating group discussions, employees feel valued and willingly participate in organization improvement initiatives. Working together to establish short-term and long-term goals provides the opportunity for participants to experience small victories that build momentum. All of these actions help to provide a new sense of purpose and an opportunity for the members to push for new and better ways of operating.

> *Working together to establish short-term and long-term goals provides the opportunity for participants to experience small victories that build momentum.*

5. BE OPEN AND TRANSPARENT TO ENCOURAGE THE SAME

I called the CEO a few months into this project after realizing that it was evolving into a much larger initiative than originally discussed. I pointed out to him that there were likely many more experienced Organizational Development practitioners to lead the company through this process. His response was entirely encouraging, explaining that he felt I was the best fit for many reasons. While he definitely did not expect this project to evolve to where it was, he was thrilled with the progress and believed that this was exactly how to move forward.

This early exchange, in my opinion, set the stage for more honest and open conversations going forward between the CEO and myself, and with all of the leaders. The CEO in many instances showed great humility by sharing when he was unsure about the best way to proceed or by admitting when he had not handled a situation in the best light. There were setbacks and at the same time the leaders developed an environment that encouraged them to openly discuss events, both positive and negative. By sharing how they handled situations, they all participated and shared their personal perspectives, strengthening the collective intelligence.

> *This early exchange, in my opinion,*
> *set the stage for more honest and open conversations*
> *going forward ...*

6. When Top Management Embraces the Initiatives They Model the Way for the Rest of the Organization

Initially, the leaders were not working as a team so the rest of the organization followed suit; correcting this was the first step on the journey. I collected data and feedback from all of the leaders and then shared a summary with them so that they participated in reviewing and interpreting the results. This first collaborative experience was so positive and insightful from the perspective of all the participants that the CEO realized it was important for the leadership team to meet regularly. He scheduled monthly meetings from that point forward and asked me to facilitate.

The leadership team quickly realized that one of the main reasons the divisions were operating in silos was because the company had no overarching strategy in place. They were slow to realize the huge influence they personally exerted over the culture and the way things got done. If they wanted to improve the company's operations, the place to begin the change was with them; that was a hard lesson to learn. Especially in the beginning I remember hearing several comments such as "they need to change," speaking of their divisions as separate from themselves and as if the leaders had little influence on the way the work got done. As they gained awareness of their personal impact, the behavior of the leadership team began to shift.

> *... the place to begin the change was with them ...*

Stories were shared in the leadership meetings about how leaders were reaching out to each other in between meetings to resolve issues. In addition, leaders were enthused to share stories of employees in their divisions actively working with employees in other units to help meet a customer's request. This sharing of experiences at the leadership level created a positive momentum that encouraged further change. The leadership team, and particularly the CEO, learned that influence can be more powerful than control; they set the example and inspired the employees. That approach ignited a new energy and a sense of hope beyond what the most carefully thought-out and well-meaning directives can achieve.

7. Use a Cross-Company Employee Team to Help Further Develop a Practical Strategy

The leadership team realized that to achieve better results, it was on them to define a new direction for the company. I supported them in formulating a vision, mission, and list of core values. While the experience of developing these guiding principles was exciting and critical, we discovered that the most difficult part was developing the abstract concepts into an actionable plan. The CEO shared with me that while he had experience creating and rolling out strategic plans at former employers, this was the first time he created a plan that evolved from an abstract strategic vision. This was a new experience for all of us. The leadership agreed to form a team of representatives from each division. The criteria for nomination to this team included being perceived as influential and respected within the larger community of employees. This team served as a sounding board for the leadership as they created the new direction for the organization. This provided both a broader viewpoint and a practical perspective, and was a tremendous benefit for the effort.

The leadership team, and particularly the CEO, were somewhat uncomfortable with the idea that the company strategy be shared with a cross-company team before it was fully evolved. A frequent comment early on was that other employees (meaning outside of the leadership) did not have the knowledge to develop a strategy. It was exciting to see that opinion change through several months of meeting with the cross-company team. A level of trust and respect grew with each interaction as the passion, intelligence, knowledge, and front line perspective of the employees was given a forum. The leaders came to realize that this process was not about giving up authority; instead it was about making use of valuable resources.

8. NOTICE HOW PATTERNS OF BEHAVIOR ARE GETTING IN THE WAY OF ADVANCING THE ORGANIZATION

Many times the leaders and employees are so deeply entrenched in their environment that they fail to see unhealthy patterns of behavior; particularly those to which they are directly contributing. I found an important role for me to play is simply sharing what I noticed and have them reflect or think about how these patterns are impacting the overall workplace. This can help provide the perspective and impetus to change to a better way of operating.

Simple examples of this early on included holding meetings without agendas or expected outcomes, failing to follow-up with minutes, or a lack of tracking agreed upon action plans. In addition, there seemed to be too many instances of employees elevating problems to their managers and the CEO. Employees in several departments did not seem to feel empowered or equipped to resolve issues where they occurred. Perhaps most significantly, I heard stories of a handful of employees whose behaviors were negatively impacting the operations of the company without any follow-up. During countless interviews, I heard stories shared about how these few individuals had repeatedly negatively impacted the operations due to poor planning, miscommunication of customer deadlines, and avoidance of established protocols. The repercussions of the work of these few individuals caused the shared resources such as warehouse and field operations to be stretched to the point that many other staff members were impacted.

The CEO referred to these difficult people-related issues as the touchy feely stuff and it took quite a bit of coaching to help him explore and then discover how critical it is to deal with these issues head-on. Letting these negative patterns continue without intervening was impeding company progress and also eroding the morale of the employees that were repeatedly impacted. Helping him to consider these issues from a systems perspective and how the behaviors were impacting the overall operations empowered him to gain a new awareness.

I recall one breakthrough that occurred during a coaching conversation with the CEO. During this conversation, the CEO acknowledged that providing feedback and confronting poor performance was difficult for him. Because of this acknowledged difficulty he realized that he wanted to commit time to preparing for the conversation by thinking through the desired outcomes, planning the talking points, and practicing before ultimately delivering the message.

9. THE ANSWERS WILL COME IF GIVEN THE RIGHT FORUM

Throughout this long-term project, I also served as a consultant diagnosing outcomes of six different divisions of the organization. Typically, this included a multi-phased approach that involved collecting data and comments from a broad cross section of the division employees, collecting relevant data about the division's performance, and then summarizing the results and sharing them in collaborative planning sessions.

The Sales and Operations Group stood out as benefiting the most from this process and their progress is particularly exciting. This division was identified by the leadership team from the start as clearly having the most problems in the entire organization, with sales and profitability in a downward spiral for multiple years. The division was repeatedly raised as a topic of concern at the leadership meetings; none of the leaders seemed to have ideas for how to improve. The CEO was the acting manager and even he felt that he was unable to influence the direction of the group.

The sales estimators had gained the reputation of rejecting new initiatives, working primarily in their individual self-interests, and lacking an understanding of the individual impact they had on the rest of the division. The individuals competed against each other and often times had adversarial relationships with their internal customers. There was no department leader, so the CEO filled in as the default leader even though he had little available time to commit to them.

Outdated incentives encouraged individual effort and seemed to discourage cooperation. I proposed applying the same diagnostic approach that was applied to the leadership team, and the CEO agreed. I collected feedback from the entire commercial sales and operations division: sales estimators, field supervision, warehouse, and operations. I first conducted a confidential survey with the whole group (at the recommendation of the CEO), then scheduled face-to-face interviews with each member. A five-year history of sales, profit margins, and backlog was collected to help provide more perspective. As with earlier diagnostics, a group meeting was held with all of the participants in order to share the summary, and the participants were encouraged to interpret the data.

At that first big meeting I distinctly remember hearing many of the participants saying things like, "the company needs to do…" this or that, and "they (meaning other people) need to change". During this initial meeting, we used an activity that provides three rounds of group discussions that builds on each previous round. In the first round, the team reviews the summary of their collective feedback, the second round encourages the team members to interpret the results, and during the last round the group is challenged to prioritize the themes and topics requiring the most attention.

As a result of the lively discussions, it was evident there was a lot of work to be done. By the end of the first meeting the group came to the conclusion that there were three main themes to be addressed and almost all of the employees volunteered to work on one of the teams. This was groundbreaking in itself and completely surprised the CEO, who expected an apathetic response. It was encouraging to see many of the employees leave that meeting encouraged by the fact that their coworkers had expressed many of the same concerns and desired results.

Three teams were created comprised of participants from all functions in the division, and they began working collaboratively for what was essentially the first time. Team leaders were elected and they drafted charter plans which were shared at the first team meetings, empowering the members to have input and align around the scope. I helped to facilitate many of the meetings and it was a great experience to observe the interactions and watch the teams develop and mature. I saw meaningful conversations occur in the team meetings between individuals that had worked in the same building for over 20 years and had failed to really talk or listen to one another.

After several weeks of the teams meeting individually, we called the whole group together to check-in and share progress. The change in attitude was apparent. The team members gained a better awareness of how each person's actions affects the group's' operations as a whole, and they also seemed to realize that they had the opportunity to actively participate in creating the results and the environment they wanted.

> *... opportunity to actively participate in creating the results*

10. CLEARLY DEFINING PROJECT OUTCOMES AND INDICATORS OF SUCCESS UPFRONT PROVIDES A CLEAR FOCUS

It was a rocky road of progress for the sales and operations team meetings and adjustments were made. A few months into the initiative, the CEO expressed frustration that one of the teams was slow to make progress. He had not attended the individual team meetings so instead relied on mixed feedback from some of the team members. As he was sharing his frustration it was clear that the CEO had expectations about the team's efforts he had failed to share. As a result, the CEO was asking for individual feedback against unknown expectations. Because the overall initiative had been insufficiently defined in measurable and objective terms at the divisional level, the team members were evaluating progress with respect to their own individual and varied standards.

In order to help with better alignment, the CEO shared what he wanted the group to accomplish first with the three team leaders to get their input and understanding. He then shared his carefully thought out vision by including the behaviors and outcomes he wanted the group to work towards at the next collective meeting. This transparency of defining the outcomes helped to align the efforts of the three teams and brought a sharper focus to what they were collectively working towards. By providing this level of guidance, while still empowering them to own the process, the members actively participated, gained new skills and confidence, and helped to build momentum as they progressed.

> *This transparency of defining the outcomes helped to align the efforts ... and brought a sharper focus to what they were collectively working towards.*

CONCLUSION

This company's story will continue to be a work in progress; the journey has provided an eye-opening and challenging learning experience. I hope that by sharing my insights it will help inspire others, especially those new to the fields of Organizational Development or coaching. I acquired a new perspective through this journey that both helped build my awareness and confidence and also helped me to realize what I offer. I see possibilities and I help the organizations I work with to see the prospects of a better future. I also believe that this is what the field of OD and the coaching profession is all about; we see the potential for our clients, our communities, and the world at large, and we help them to realize their capabilities.

Kelly Gangl is founder of Connect-to-thrive Business Coaching, LLC and she provides 20+ years of human resources and organization development leadership experience. Kelly earned a B.S. Degree in Human Resource Management from Ohio State University and actively maintains the SPHR Certification. She graduated with a Master's Degree in Organization Development from Bowling Green State University and is Certified as a Professional Coach through the Center for Coaching Certification.

Since December of 2014 Kelly has been providing organization and leadership consulting and coaching services. Prior to her foray into self-employment, Kelly served as Vice President of Human Resources for Herman & Kittle Properties, Inc. Over the course of her career, Kelly has served in key human resource leadership roles for small, medium, and large size employers in several industries including medical manufacturing, real estate development, direct mail, construction trades, and student loan services.

Kelly is committed to helping businesses connect their people with the overall company strategies and is passionate about coaching organizations, leaders, individuals, and teams to their full potential.

www.Connect-to-Thrive.com

THE HR LEADER'S TRANSITION TO COACH
Cheryl Knight

LISTENING, QUESTIONS, AND EXPECTATIONS

Human Resource professionals are often asked to coach employees, both individual contributors and leaders. The actual goal may be to give them some feedback that their manager has trouble delivering, or the manager has delivered feedback and now thinks the individual will understand better with another perspective. Sometimes they have received feedback and nothing changed, so the manager wants you to help them. Spur them along. Fix them, please? You are HR, so that's what you do, right?

I recall one such situation with a leader who I'll call Jim. Jim was a high ranking senior leader within my client department. His military background provided the expertise and technical knowledge required to run the department. Operationally, the department was successful. Despite his credentials and achievement of the departmental goals, Jim related poorly with his employees. He came across a bit gruff and sometimes made people angry. As his HR leader, I was asked to interview his peers and some of his direct reports who were also managers. Having done so, I was armed with lots of feedback and then went about preparing to deliver the feedback and the coaching.

After consolidating my notes and finding the themes of the feedback, I was ready.

We sat down and I shared the process I used and what I had discovered. Jim was polite. Well, at least he listened to the comments and my conclusion: his relationships were limited. This was a problem that was expected to be fixed. I then proceeded to tell Jim what he could do to accomplish this goal. "You need to change," I told him. Jim left that meeting in a pleasant enough way and then a few months later he left the company. He had failed. Or had I?

Perhaps you've experienced a similar situation. What I now know is that I failed to listen, I failed to ask the right questions, and I had unrealistic expectations. I also failed to really listen to the executive that asked me to provide the coaching, to the individuals providing their feedback on Jim, or Jim himself during our meeting. I failed to ask the executive the right questions, I failed to ask the peers and direct reports the right questions, and I certainly failed to ask Jim, well, hardly anything! I was unsure of the executive's ultimate expectations of either me or Jim. I went into the interviews with my own expectations and I unclear myself and thus unclear with Jim about what to expect from this experience.

As a rising professional in the HR field, I wanted to succeed, I wanted to prove I had what it takes, plus I wanted to show leadership that I could help others succeed, grow, and develop! I was providing direction, giving feedback, encouraging others, helping them with their development, telling them what they could do to improve or overcome their challenges. I was all about helping in a way I thought was coaching.

In these situations, the direction, feedback, encouragement, and advice I provided was based entirely on what I thought they needed to do and my ideas were based on my perceptions. There was little said or done regarding what they wanted and what was important to them. I failed to explore how or even if they wanted to approach their challenge or how they wanted to grow their skills to achieve their goals. I have found that helping or coaching people to my expectations rarely results in lasting change.

In my failure, rather than shying away from coaching my passion led me to transition from the HR Generalist work to focus solely on leadership development. Now I design and deliver programs to accelerate leaders' growth. I help people that want to be successful. I work with them because they have an expectation to get better, they want this change. I stopped trying to fix anyone.

> *I stopped trying to fix anyone.*

Like many of you who strive to help others get better, I provide the structure and the process for development. Perhaps you have created opportunities for self-awareness or taught classes to develop leadership skills. You may have helped others write a development plan to ensure success in achieving their goal.

Even in sharing all this knowledge and feedback on their development, it can be frustrating when leaders fail to exhibit the changes we want to see. Why don't they just do what we tell them? They would be amazingly successful if they would just apply the knowledge we've imparted, the skills we've taught them, or the behavioral changes suggested. After all, they asked for it!

It became apparent to me that to be a coach, I was going to have to change a few things:
- How I listen
- The questions I ask
- The expectations I have for others

We'll cover all three of these. Let's begin with how to change our approach to listening.

LISTENING

Listening is a big responsibility in many professions, including the HR leader's role. We listen to employees talk about problems with their managers, personal situations, and their concerns. "I don't think my manager is being fair;" "I'm having trouble with child care;" or "I've done all the training, but I'm still not getting promoted; what do I do?" All these conversations spur us into action to resolve the issues, provide information on resources, or give them advice or counseling, often mistakenly referred to as coaching.

With these type of issues, it is easy to take action. You listen to the person and then work to resolve their concern or give them some advice. The action or advice is often based upon our own frames of reference, what we see or think of as important. Here is the challenge: how often do your recommended actions support your own sense of success? How often do you limit what works and doesn't work to your own experiences? We often draw upon things we have learned when helping others with similar problems. Rarely do I recall intently listening to the person with the problem to fully understand their perspective, the uniqueness of their situation, or the type of language they used to describe their concern.

When working with someone as a coach, our listening skills require a greater depth than that required to be successful as a HR or leadership development professional. Coaches listen to what is being said, as well as how it is said and the reasons it is being said.

- What is their learning style and personality?
- How are they perceiving it?

- How many positive, proactive words versus limiting, negative words are being used?
- What is their ownership of what they are discussing?
- How optimistic and sincere are they about making changes?
- What is not being said?

Each of these characteristics or aspects of communication are important to clarify what you hear and can guide how you engage with the person, what questions you ask, and how you move forward in helping them.

Active Listening is one of the eleven core competencies the International Coach Federation (ICF) has in its credentialing criteria. The ICF provides examples of what is required in Active Listening. This can be helpful to those wanting to increase their level of competence and skill in this area. An example of active listening the ICF encourages is listening to see how you can help the client gain clarity and perspective on their situation, goals, or challenges. Being totally engaged in listening to the client's story is good only if you as coach are able to maintain an awareness of what the client is experiencing. As a coach you want to find opportunities to probe, challenge, or hold up a mirror (the metaphorical mirror is used to help the client see what you as receiver of their message are seeing). If you become so engaged in what the client is saying that it feels like you are the recipient of a fascinating story, you are missing the active part of listening.

Three practices to enhance your listening skills include:
1. Using all your senses
2. Rephrasing
3. Reflecting

Let's explore all three practices in the next section.

USING ALL YOUR SENSES

This takes intention and practice and is likely the most challenging skill to develop, so let's begin here. With active listening, you are listening to the words plus you are listening for the tone and the type of language. You are aware of the emotions you are sensing from the client as well as your own reaction. All of these inform and guide you.

The language the client uses is very informative and provides direction to the questions you will use. Following are several examples. One challenge as coach is to understand where they are, which can be anywhere on the continuum of beliefs.

You can determine their comfort with the known or unknown by listening to how they describe the things they have done, experienced, or want to do. How are they different or similar in nature? What is their interest in doing things in a variety of ways or differently? How open are they to moving beyond what they know or have experienced?

If the client is speaking in either global or detailed language, you can get a sense of their style or preferences for how they think about and approach things. What is the level of information they share? You can listen for a preference of having options in how they approach things or a preference for procedure and step by step instructions.

Other aspects of understanding the client include listening to how they describe their goals or aspirations. Where are they focused? For example, some describe what they want to do and others focus on what they don't want or the negative. How do they explain their motivation? What is the source of the motivation? What is their preference for initiating action versus waiting for something else to happen or for someone else to do something? How empowering are their beliefs?

REPHRASING AND REFLECTING

Both rephrasing and reflecting require total commitment. In order to rephrase what you are hearing, you must be listening. If you fail to actively engage it is easy to let thoughts wander. When you are actively listening you are able to rephrase or describe what you have just heard. When you reflect, you are sharing what the emotion or feeling is that you are sensing. Doing both of these helps the client know that you hear what is being said and that you are tuned in to how they feel.

Practicing these listening skills establishes trust and a deeper connection with the client. Significantly important to your overall comprehension of what you are hearing is being certain your interpretation is correct. When you rephrase a thought you just heard or reflect a feeling and get it wrong, this gives the client a chance to correct your understanding.

Through the use of rephrasing and reflecting you will gain clarity and a greater understanding that what you think you heard is indeed what the client is saying and feeling.

When you are actively listening and are able to pick up the subtleties described, you gain a firmer foundation of understanding.

By rephrasing and reflecting the client experiences that you are listening and truly get their point of view. An additional benefit for clients is that when you rephrase and reflect it helps them achieve clarity in their own thinking.

> *By rephrasing and reflecting the client experiences that you are listening and truly get their point of view.*

How you listen, how well you listen, and the understanding you gain as you listen are what leads to the way you approach questioning.

QUESTIONS

The HR professional's role requires a lot of question asking. We ask interview questions to help us learn about someone and what they have to offer the company. We ask investigation questions to gather facts, feelings, and specific details to understand what happened that led to an investigation. We ask questions of the business managers to understand what their needs are and what strategic goals they want to achieve so that we can help them determine the right number of employees, organizational structure, or pay grade for a job.

HR professionals go into data collection mode a lot and all this data is filtered through expertise, knowledge, and the policies and systems utilized. The answers to our questions inform the responses and solutions we provide to the business. We ask questions to be able to solve problems. The HR professional gathers relevant data by asking skillfully designed questions that then inform our decision.

In the role of coach, the questions asked are significant. The endgame is very different. The coach asks questions to discover what the client wants, their options, barriers, opportunities, resources, and what is important to them. Coaches ask what has been working, what feedback clients have received, challenges, and how the client wants to move forward. We ask questions to help clients learn about themselves.

> *We ask questions to help clients learn about themselves.*

An understanding of the client's communication style, how they view the world, their situation, and what they want in the different aspects of their life informs coaching questions and client exploration. Most importantly, coaches want to understand the client's belief in their ability to effect change in their situation, their approach, and in their own behavior to then effectively support them moving forward. Asking the right questions helps the client be aware of pertinent information throughout the coaching process.

As to the endgame being different: the goal of asking questions of a client rather than an employee in a work situation is to coach them through a process that empowers them to proactively handle their own challenges. In the HR role when you are advising an employee it is likely the result of a business problem that has surfaced. The individual that hires a coach on their own is getting the coach of their own choice. The endgame is to achieve a human solution, specific to a particular person. The agenda is different so the questions are different.

The ICF evaluates Powerful Questioning as part of the credentialing exam and describes Powerful Questioning as the ability to ask questions that gain the most benefit for the client. That is important: the coach asks questions for the benefit of the client. Questions can support client learning around how they arrived at their current situation and challenges. Questions help clients understand what they hope to accomplish and what is preventing them from achieving their goals. When as a coach we do a good job of listening, we are in a better position to ask powerful coaching questions.

One of the most effective ways to ask questions is to align your style of asking with the client's linguistics style preference: visual, auditory, or kinesthetic. The basics of the styles are this:
- Visual language paints a picture.
- Auditory language references how things sound.
- Kinesthetic is about action or how things feel.

While many people have a combination of styles, we all have a predominate style that can be recognized. When listening to a client the difference can be as follows:
- "I can *see* what my future holds." - visual
- "I can *say* what my future holds." - auditory
- "I can *sense* what my future holds." - kinesthetic

Powerful Questioning uses this awareness to phrase questions in the same linguistic style as the client. Whether you asking to create awareness or challenging the client to think differently, you will be speaking in a relatable way. Adjust your word choice to the client's preferences:

- Visual clients prefer to see you use visual words such as: picture, view, focus, or appears.
- Auditory clients prefer hearing words like: sounds, volume, hear, and tell.
- Kinesthetic clients will relate to the words: feel, grasp, in touch, and reshape.

The visual client that is imagining what their future holds may respond more easily to questions such as:
- Picture yourself in five years; what do you see yourself doing?
- Paint a picture of how you will _____; what does it look like?
- Draw a map of your plan; what are the stops you want to make along the way? What will those stops look like?

When working with an auditory style client who is defining what their future holds, use words that denote listening or the use of the hearing sense. Some examples are:
- Describe your future in a way that makes you proud.
- What are you saying to yourself about your future?
- What words describe your ideal future?
- Pretend you are you in the future; what are the sounds you hear around you?

For the kinesthetic client, it is all about touch and feeling. Questions that use their preferred style include:
- How do you feel when you reflect on your future?

- Envision yourself firmly positioned in the future. Where are you? What is supporting you? What things can you reach out and touch?
- In reshaping your future, where do you want to begin?

There are many different coaching models used throughout the world. All use questions to further the goal of helping the client achieve their desired outcome. All clients have different objectives and goals, all calling for a different line of questioning. One thing that adds value in coaching models and for clients is when the questions look like, sound like, and feel like they are in the client's language. This is also where the deeper, personal connection in coaching begins.

> *... use questions to further the goal of helping the client achieve their desired outcome.*

EXPECTATIONS

I think the expectations of HR Leaders are much the same as those of the business leader when dealing with performance matters. We expect the employee to listen and take action on the feedback, advice, or direction we are giving. When it comes to people's livelihoods, they usually do their best to take action. At the same time, it may or may not work out as well as expected.

A lack of follow-through or action may occur for several reasons:

1. They may not agree with the feedback and therefore are not open to taking action on the subsequent advice or direction.
2. Even if they accept the feedback, they may neither understand nor agree with the advice or direction given.
3. They believe they can correct the problem on their own.
4. They may try their own approach without ongoing support.
5. They go back to their old pre-feedback behaviors or habits.
6. Sadly, many times the feedback message is so muddled it is challenging to translate into any specific action.

In these instances, the employee often continues to demonstrate the undesired behaviors and either progressive discipline ensues, the employee realizes their approach is unappreciated and leaves, or the manager moves on, leaving the problem behavior for the next unsuspecting manager.

When results fall short of our expectations it is frustrating. As HR professionals we either have to continue counseling the employee, advise the manager on how to work with the employee, or perform progressive discipline. Either way, no one is happy. We are failing the employee and the manager is dissatisfied with having to spend energy on a performance issue. We are discouraged and may feel unsuccessful in our ability to help an employee. Ultimately the organization suffers.

As a coach in a sponsored or non-sponsored arrangement, our expectations are different from that of HR Leader. Our expectations are that the individual we are coaching is open to the coaching process, that they actively want to make some behavior changes, and that they will be an active participant. Sometimes we do work to generate that open and willing interest before starting.

Once a coaching engagement has begun, the expectations are that the client will work the process, share their thoughts, discuss their goals, and explore how they can achieve them. We expect that when they commit to a specific action they will indeed take that action. These are the expectations to which we serve the client as an accountability partner. It will involve additional coaching skills to help our client make progress. Please note: it can be foolhardy to think any individual will easily make behavioral changes and simply follow the process without challenges.

When it comes to expectations, it is also important to manage the client's expectations. They, too, may hold unrealistic expectations similar to that of employee rather than client. Sometimes a new client will expect the coach to provide the answers instead of guiding them to discover and choose their own answer. I realized with one individual I was coaching that I failed to manage these expectations clearly enough at the onset. I will call her Sue. Sue shared that she was disappointed I failed to provide enough leadership solutions for her, stating, "I thought you had more leadership knowledge than you do." She was expecting me to simply tell her what to do; she wanted an expert advisor. My approach was to help Sue discover her own solutions. Even when we brainstormed possible approaches, I thought I was clear that my ideas were only some of the ideas and that she was in charge of deciding what action she wanted to take. In retrospect, if I had spent more time at the beginning, when establishing the agreement, we could have fleshed this out. Clarifying and agreeing on the role of a coach to ensure we had the same expectations would have improved the coaching relationship.

Clear expectations start with the initial conversation and are formalized in an agreement. With clear expectations at the beginning, coaching has purpose and the outcome is enhanced.

> *Clear expectations start with your initial conversation and are formalized in an agreement.*

SUMMARY

Making the transition from HR Leader to Coach, whether you are making a career change or want to transition within your organization, it is possible to achieve success if you continue to refine your skills.

As I continue my transition to Coach, there are many skills I will continue to develop. Through my early coaching experiences, I have learned that to be a better coach, the areas of biggest challenge and greatest learning have been the three we just covered:

- How I listen
- The questions I ask
- The expectations I have for others

By continuing to focus on these three key areas and participating in continuing education, I know I will, and you can too, build a strong foundation for future coaching engagements.

Cheryl Knight is a Coach and Developer of Leaders within the business and retail environment. She has over 25 years in the Human Resource profession with over half of her experience in training, coaching, facilitation, and leadership development. Cheryl has led change management, employee relations, diversity, leadership development, retention, and talent acquisition efforts. Cheryl has worked with a variety of businesses, public and private, as well as multinational and small startup companies.

Cheryl's focus is to help leaders learn more about themselves through assessments and feedback, gain clarity on their goals and aspirations, and then provide a process to accelerate their growth and development.

Cheryl graduated from Texas A&M Corpus Christi with a Bachelor of Arts degree in Sociology. She is certified as a Professional in Human Resources through the HR Certification Institute and as a Certified Professional Coach through the Center for Coaching Certification and Marshall Goldsmith Stakeholder Centered Coaching. Additionally, Cheryl has certifications in the Myers Briggs Type Instrument, the EQ-I 2.0 and EQ-I 360 as well as the CPI 260.

www.linkedin.com/in/coachcherylk

AFFIRMATION FOR SUSTAINABLE CHANGE
Juanita Bulloch

The journey to coaching and applying coaching for sustainable change has included many ups and downs in my life. The resulting insights and thoughts are shared here because by sharing I reinforce my learning and I also encourage you in your learning.

SUCCESS IMPACTED BY NEGATIVE THINKING

What are your dreams and goals? What is holding you back? What undermines your plans? What fuels procrastination? Where does the resistance come from? What is this enemy of the best of intentions? What robs you of self-confidence? What sabotages your diet plan? What drains your energy? What keeps you awake at night? What fuels your stress? What keeps you hanging on to something that no longer works for you? How are you thinking about your possibilities?

Listening to the stories others tell of the obstacles and challenges they overcame and how they are now living an incredibly abundant joyous life, better than they ever imagined, my challenges seem miniscule. At the same time, the reality is negative thoughts still hold us back and keep us in that place of less than. Sometimes we even become comfortable with our negativity because it is the known, a familiar old habit. Stepping into positive thought and facing the possibilities of the unknown brings up fear, fear of the change involved by moving from the unconscious to the conscious.

A note: this chapter is the application of the research so you are encouraged to use the information. If you want to review the research it is readily available by doing a search online.

Science is showing that positive thinking such as gratitude and compassion supports our making changes and has a positive impact on our health. Becoming aware of words, really hearing what is said, and being conscious of word choice are the first steps in making changes because changing language changes outcomes. Using positive words, present tense, and active verbs really changes the feel of a message.

> *Science is showing that positive thinking such as gratitude and compassion supports our making changes and has a positive impact on our health.*

A study that also gives hope showed that mice, exposed to a particular behavior in one generation, transfer the tendency toward that behavior in the subsequent generation. This is also showing up in humans with the propensity of children learning and using technology a prime example. Similar situations exist in cultures where anger and fear or superiority and separateness are experienced in everyday life as compared to the potential for experiencing equality, oneness, and individual uniqueness.

Research from coaching professionals, medical professionals, and others confirm that negative language requires more time for processing a message than does a message delivered in a positive framework. A person using positive language is viewed as more credible. Think about someone viewed as charismatic versus someone considered toxic. What do you notice about their language and interactions? The charismatic person is viewed as far more desirable to be around and viewed as more successful personally and professionally because of their positive language and behavior.

Brain scans are being used to show the impact of positive language and interactions in the brain. The field of neuroplasticity is growing and showing that we grow new neuropathways when habits and beliefs are changed. Affirmations are supportive of changing habits and beliefs. Photographic equipment is now sensitive enough to capture energy in photos and the energy fields of plants show certain changes when interacting with humans expressing positive emotions. Human interactions that are positive show a different photo than negative interactions.

The point of sharing the connection to science is for showing there is scientific evidence supporting the use of positivity. Words and language are an important vehicle for exposing and incorporating positivity in our lives and supporting positive changes in thoughts, beliefs, and behavior. With this awareness comes the potential for changing the way we talk to ourselves, interact with others, and just imagine the impact if we applied the same concept when educating children!

Scientists are now showing that our thoughts change the chemistry and environment in our bodies causing changes in the cells in our bodies. When negative words and thoughts are used, cortisol is released resulting in stress and disease; positive words and thoughts cause the body to release different chemicals resulting in health and wellness.

In 2015 the International Coach Federation changed their code of ethics so it reflects positive language and states what is desired, versus previously stating what *not to do*, in the performance as an ICF member or credentialed coach.

Choosing Positivity

When beginning change, it seems a battle is being waged: which wins - the old negative habit or the new positive habit? Relate this to the story of two forces fighting inside of us, one negative, one positive. Which one wins? The one you feed! Feed your mind positive words and affirmations and the positive wins.

A piece of the puzzle for sustaining positive thinking is practice and repetition. The changes affect our physical bodies and require the action be repeated enough that the body and behavior perceive it as the norm or habit. The sequence is word – chemistry – brain activity – feeling – behavior – internal and external environment – results. This process happens whether the word is positive or negative, and has very different outcomes. Positive affirmation is key for sustainable positive change.

When a worry, fear, or negativity shows up, write the description of what you are experiencing. Then rewrite it carefully in a positive format expressing what you want for your experience. Use this positive statement as an affirmation. Using positive language is affirming. An affirmation clarifies and gets to the point by making a statement of being or desired being. Keeping the statement short increases its power. Present tense language serves to ground and keep one in the now with a positive focus.

> *Using positive language is affirming.*

For an affirmation to be effective, our logical mind must believe the statement. Changing a limiting, negative belief starts with choosing words that are positive and inspiring when stating what is desired as the new belief. Key for the new becoming believable is repetition of the statement of the belief supported by behavior and actions reflecting the new reality. Coaching is supportive of the process by working with the client in a coaching relationship through the process of identifying goals and actions that move the client toward their new belief.

Believing an ideal is possible may start with healing of self, forgiveness of self and/or others, an openness for receiving love, support, caring, money, companionship, blessings, change, positive feedback, nutrition, and the list goes on. This is supported by an openness for life, doing your best, expecting the best, and believing in abundance. Expressing gratitude for everything in life, tangible and intangible. Taking care of yourself first supports giving to others. Remember the flight attendant's safety message: Put your oxygen mask on first.

Writing affirmations is about seeing yourself as capable. Saying "I am xxxxxxxx" where xxxxxxxx is a positive word or words, is saying I am whole and capable of making a choice. Coach training with the Center for Coaching Certification includes the competency of creating awareness. This means recognizing and challenging when people say statements that equate to 'I am not capable' because if they say it they believe it. For example, saying 'I can't do that' or 'I always mess up' is playing helpless or succumbing to limiting beliefs about ourselves. Uncovering limiting beliefs is an invitation to write a positive affirmation. The process of finding powerful positive words includes digging deep to uncover the basis of the negative thoughts and choosing change, leading to greater understanding plus acceptance of self and others.

Resistance is the result of failing to take responsibility for choices or viewing a choice as letting someone else decide.

Passive behavior is helping someone else be in charge instead of expressing personal preferences or desires. Creating buy-in and commitment means seeing it as supporting growth and life purpose which in turn results in helping others. Identifying what is wanted and then putting it into a seeing, hearing, and feeling language makes it real, plus gives a map for making choices along the way. When reaching a choice point or a fork in the path, ask: How does this advance me in the direction I want? How is it a wise use of my resources?

> *Identifying what is wanted and then putting it into a seeing, hearing, and feeling language makes it real ...*

Perhaps you are thinking: okay, now that I have this insight, how do I move forward given I am in the middle of all these choices I made earlier? Without a clean slate from which to start, how do I move forward from here? It is possible to make new choices, develop your positive beliefs, and move in new directions and positive affirmations will support your process.

TAKING THE CHALLENGE

One of my coaches asked me when I was going to begin listening to what I wanted, my story as a positive affirmation. Specifically, I have my story as a recording in my voice describing my ideal life. I hesitated with an answer, then said,

"I don't believe the story." My coach asked permission to push back; I agreed. Her questions to me included: "How willing are you to test whether or not it works? What do you have to lose by listening for thirty days? What if it does work?"

So begins my experience using affirmations. Initially the purpose was building self-confidence. In the process of writing and using affirmations, limiting beliefs were exposed along with the awareness of the benefits of change. Expression of new beliefs, with confidence, resulted in both change and actions for moving forward toward an ideal life.

> *Expression of new beliefs, with confidence, resulted in both change and actions for moving forward toward an ideal life.*

Using an affirmation in the form of my story easily becomes a habit. The good feeling resulting from listening encourages using it every night. When I get in bed at night and my head hits the pillow, I reach for the on switch of the recorder! Shortly, I am asleep. Hearing my voice use positive words describing my ideal life is very calming and relaxing. Listening to myself talking actually shuts down my mind, easily lulling me to sleep. I am blocked from listening to the limiting thoughts in my mind while listening to myself say my story in positive language. My personal experiment is supporting what science is discovering. As an added benefit, it is easier to listen to positive language than negative.

Confidence increases as a result of using an affirmation in the form of my story. The positive language, expressions of moving forward, and achieving what is desired as expressed in an affirmation build confidence. Affirmations benefit any area of life that is expressed in the affirmation.

> *Confidence increases as a result of using an affirmation ...*

How does one address something they want to improve? Use my procrastination as an example. I decided to write a chapter for this book, and all the negative stuff started coming up. I checked my story recording and even completing the writing was missing. Because this is important to me, it was time for a revision to have an updated affirmation story.

An important note about updating your affirmation is writing so that the change in the story is pertinent for your life and remains meaningful for some time. There are specific goals that once achieved remain a positive force by reminding us of achievements, offering encouragement and inspiration.

For me, I added, "I easily write three plus pages each day as I am focused and productive because creative thoughts flow naturally which means expression of my thoughts and knowledge is from my mind and heart so now I imagine my name in print as an author realizing I feel inspired and confident for continuing writing so I say to myself 'awesome message'."

When using this tool, I consciously write so it includes visual, auditory, and kinesthetic words. Really making an affirmation come alive includes experiencing the story three dimensionally – with all the senses. How do we as humans experience the world? Through our senses. Involvement of our senses of sight, hearing, touch, feeling, taste, and smell bring our affirmations alive, causing us experiencing them as real, and encouraging action.

Writing the affirmation is important. Hearing the affirmation every day is critical for changing thoughts and beliefs. Changing requires repetitive, consistent thought and action.

> *Changing requires repetitive, consistent thought and action.*

SELF-COACHING WITH AFFIRMATIONS

Because of the title of this chapter in this book, Affirmation for Sustainable Change, one may immediately think of using affirmations when coaching a client. As a coach, I ask myself how I will use coaching skills and affirmations in the conversations I have with myself during the day. The recording of my story as an affirmation is a conversation I have with myself while sleeping. In my story, I state what I want as my ideal in areas of my life I perceive as important. So how do I use this during the day when the mental chatter starts? One option is choosing specific statements from the recording and rewrite them in short sentences addressing a current situation. Then, if the negative thoughts begin and I become aware, I begin repeating the one line affirmations and regain my positive attitude for what I want.

Other tricks are writing affirmations on sticky notes, on mirrors with dry erase markers, and being creative with placement and pictures. The tendency is to stop seeing something that is in front of us all the time so if you notice negativity creeping into thoughts and beliefs, maybe it is time to change the placement, change the color, or decorate the statements so you are doing something different that draws your attention.

Ever since writing a short story in seventh grade, I have had thoughts of writing fiction. Forty-five years of my life were spent working in mathematics and accounting (not exactly related to writing). When agreeing to write this chapter, excitement and opportunity clouded my clarity around my preparedness for the task. Later I asked myself, "How on earth am I going to do this?" "Use affirmations!" was my answer. What affirmations support my writing this chapter? I tell myself: I am confident in my ability to write a chapter. I am expressing my thoughts clearly and words flow easily. I am finding joy and pleasure in writing this chapter. I am appreciative of the opportunity for participating as an author in Coaching Perspectives.

AFFIRMATIONS AS A TOOL WHEN COACHING CLIENTS

One of the ways I am using affirmations with my clients is including at least one affirmation with the notes from each coaching session. The wording of the affirmation is expressing something the client referenced or stated during the session that they want or a desired outcome. This offers support for the client and verifies they are being heard. Affirmations are also a way of reminding clients of the importance of practicing positive language. It is up to the client as to how they use the affirmation. I include affirmations in my notes after verifying my client has knowledge and awareness of the value in using affirmations. Coaches, at an appropriate time during a coaching call, ask your client, "what is your knowledge or experience using affirmations?" If the answer is none, ask permission for sharing perspective and exploring possibilities using positive statements.

> *Affirmations are also a way of reminding clients of the importance of practicing positive language.*

Experiment with using the words "I am" as the beginning of affirmations as often as possible because this creates a powerful, proactive feeling. For example, close your eyes and say, "I feel confident" and then do it again saying, "I am confident". Which one seems more powerful for you? Using the "I am" brings us present and into a state of being, a very powerful place for moving forward! As stated earlier, I'm writing my affirmations in that format and sometimes it is a challenge finding the appropriate words that follow "I am". That is the fun of it and a process that often yields insights.

Challenge yourself by using each letter of the alphabet as the first letter in the word following "I am _ _ _ _ _".

APPLICATION OF PERSONAL AFFIRMATIONS

Remember earlier I mentioned expressing personal preferences as compared to simply doing to please another person? When I find myself in this circumstance, how do I make the best of the situation? By reframing my thoughts into positive statements about how I choose to view the situation. By asking myself, "what do I want from this opportunity? What is the learning for me?" and then answering these questions with positive statements I affirm my desired results.

We each have a story, one that has special meaning for ourselves. Key to moving forward is a willingness for experiencing vulnerability and sharing that story. First comes our awareness of the lesson or message in the story, seeing it as a gift or opportunity for learning. We as humans share the same challenges, they simply get expressed differently. The passion behind the story makes it special and unique. The sameness of humans is that we are each unique.

Muhammed Ali is a great example for us that affirmations work. As a newcomer in the boxing world, his statements at the time were broadcast worldwide by the news media. Many perceived him as a braggart and self-centered. Upon his recent passing, several references were made of his use of affirmations and the positive impact his life has had. His goal of being a positive example is reflected in his statements and how he lived his life.

For me, feeling safe and being in a safe environment are important. On a recent trip to my home, a six-hour drive with an overnight in a strange motel, preparation for me included saying affirmations for experiencing a safe trip. When I drove into the hotel entrance, I noticed several police cars and really did not think too much about it. Later, on my way to dinner, I realized that there were police cars everywhere in my hotel parking and the adjacent hotel. They were spending the night at my hotel. I felt safe and in a safe environment.

Affirmations materialize in many forms. Recognition of and gratitude for an affirmation coming true are keys for sustaining the change we intend. Police showing up every time I want to feel safe is not the point. The key is that I set an intention, and stated an affirmation for my desired safety. The police being there were a metaphor for my affirmation of feeling safe.

For example, a friend invited me to a social event and because of her association with the event sponsors, told me she wanted to stay at least two hours. I accepted the invitation. Very soon after, the worries started. What am I going to wear? Who do I know and how am I going to remain there two hours?! So I decided to change my focus on what may happen to what I wanted to have happen by setting the intention of meeting one new person and greeting at least one old acquaintance. That worked! The worries stopped as I looked forward to an adventure. I had a great time and met someone who offered me a coaching opportunity.

Because of the prevalence of cancer today, many of us know someone whose life has been touched by this dreaded disease. We also know there are those who survive and live long, happy lives. My experience was when a friend, Penny, was diagnosed with breast cancer. She had also seen her mother battle cancer unsuccessfully. Penny's family and friends feared the worst. Penny was the one smiling, telling jokes, and concerned for others as they visited her in the hospital and at home. Penny repeatedly told everyone that she was going to be okay. Her family supported her outlook by being cheerful and having positive conversations. Her grandchildren provided entertainment and a reason to live. Penny starts her day by creating positive affirmations, praying, and expressing gratitude for all her blessings. Within six months of the first diagnosis, she had a second surgery for removing suspicious cells in another part of her body. Penny has now been cancer free for five years! She still begins her day with gratitude and prayer.

Application of Positivity in the Workplace

This story of a small business is a great example of the power of coaching and affirmation in the turnaround of the company. It illustrates the potential impact on a business and its employees, both professionally and personally. The company was run by Joe, whose whole life was the business. Joe was the owner and president, and had been responsible for much of the growth and subsequent decline of the business to the extent that his health was declining also. Suddenly, Joe passed. The company was without a leader and succession plan. There were no family members willing or capable of taking on the role of president. The board and family asked the CFO to consider taking on the role of president. She agreed and called a meeting of all the managers, and then later set up meetings with all employees informing them of the change.

This company was founded and operated in a culture based on the president being the person making all the decisions and pretty much telling everyone what to do and when as the dictator. Because the company was in financial distress and the new president without CEO experience, the bank required the CFO turned CEO to hire consultants for helping right the ship. She chose a group of consultants that, when interviewed, talked about making financial corrections and building a team. Over the next several months, everyone, and I do mean everyone, pulled together and began operating in a new culture supported by team work. Key to the success of the transition was the feeling that everyone was valued and asked to participate in the running of the company. Problems were looked at and solutions arrived at by asking what and how to improve. Mission and vision statements were developed and assimilated throughout the company. The new CEO was being coached, meeting with the consultants, and she was coaching the employees. Everyone was focused on positive interactions, working toward getting the company righted, and in ways that also supported personal growth.

One day in an employee production meeting, a shop employee, Luke, relayed a personal incident with his wife. Luke was using the communication skills learned at work while interacting with his wife. The wife's comment was something like, "whatever you are doing at work has changed how you are at home and I like it." Hearing this story was very rewarding for the new CEO and seemed to give ideas for others practicing their improved communication skills.

Shop employees grew professionally, taking on roles of managers and supervisors. There was a focus on improvement of quality of the work and safety of employees. Employees saw the company was truly concerned for their health and well-being, and appreciated the work being produced. These actions resulted in tremendous savings in OSHA insurance and were passed to employees as bonuses. Another result of the changes was the company being named Small Manufacturer of the Year by the state Chamber of Commerce and reporting their most profitable year in the history of the company.

This company was living their affirmation. As a group they identified what they wanted in their work place, set goals, and followed up with action plans. They used positive language. The most important result was a culture change resulting in an environment where people felt safe contributing for the benefit of each other and the company. Relationships were valued and supported with effective communication. All of this made a difference in the bottom line. It also made a difference in CEO's life.

Fast forward a few years. After the CFO who became CEO retired, she again faced challenges. It was easy to get pulled into focusing on the problems and the negatives. She knew there was more out there and returned to what she had learned about coaching. She became a certified coach. In the process she was again challenged to focus on the positive. I share this story here because it is about me; I was the CFO who became the CEO. I was the one who was then challenged by a coach to listen to what I want. What do I want? I want to empower others to live a positive, proactive, and healthy life in the same way I am challenged to do and am now experiencing.

Juanita Bulloch is a Certified Master Coach through Center for Coaching Certification focusing on coaching Executives, Engineers, and Small Business Owners. With years of experience, including the presidency of a steel company, she has a keen understanding of leadership and entrepreneurship she combines with a devotion to wellness.

She holds a Bachelor of Science in Mathematics Education from the University of Georgia as well as a Bachelor of Science in Accounting and a Master of Business Administration from Francis Marion University, where the School of Business named her Outstanding Alumnus. Currently she volunteers as a math tutor for at risk students and as a mentor for entrepreneurs. Juanita is a member of the International Coach Federation.

Living her passion for nutrition, natural healing, and enjoyment of nature led Juanita to become a Reiki practitioner. Through the International Kinesiology College, she has completed Touch for Health I, II, and Metaphors, a process for clearing energy in support of a person moving toward a goal.

Juanita is a strategic partner empowering your finding answers, taking responsibility for choices, and confidently expressing new awareness and knowledge going forward.

www.JAB-Coaching.com

Made in the USA
Columbia, SC
25 April 2018